PEOPLES *of*

NORTH AMERICA

VOLUME 4

Emigrés and refugees – Guyanese

GROLIER

About This Book

Peoples of North America is a survey of the North American population at the start of the 21st century: the ethnic groups who make it up, their origins, culture, and lifestyle. The 10 volumes of the encyclopedia are organized alphabetically and describe all ethnic groups, from Afghans to West Africans. The peoples include well-established communities, relatively recent immigrants, and indigenous peoples who survive in significant numbers. Other entries also cover immigration-related and crosscultural subjects, such as intermarriage, music, and race, to help you understand how different groups have contributed to shaping modern North America.

Each entry on a specific ethnic group explains who the people are and where they live, where they came from, how they lived in the past and how they live now, and their arts, culture, and politics. Fact files and maps show the states and cities where the major communities live today. The fact files also allow you to quickly find useful information, including population figures, immigration history, languages, dominant religions, typical jobs, national foods, typical names, famous individuals, and major community organizations. The statistical data are from the U.S. and Canadian censuses. Where no date is specified, the data are based on the latest available figures: the 2000 U.S. Census or the 1996 Canadian Census.

Entries on ethnic groups all contain a box listing useful websites. There are also special boxes giving detailed information about key people, events, places, cultures, or traditions. A "See also" box at the end of each entry points you to related articles elsewhere in the encyclopedia, allowing you to further investigate topics of interest.

The index covers all 10 volumes, so it will help you trace topics throughout the set. A glossary at the end of each book gives a brief explanation of important words and concepts, and a timeline provides a chronological account of key events in the history of immigration to North America.

First Published 2003 by Grolier,
an imprint of Scholastic Library Publishing,
Old Sherman Turnpike
Danbury, Connecticut 06816

Set ISBN: 0–7172–5777–0
Volume 4 ISBN: 0–7172–5781–9

Library of Congress Cataloging-in-Publication Data

Peoples of North America
p. cm.
Includes indexes
Summary: Profiles the native and immigrant groups that have peopled North America, focusing on the modes and monitoring of immigration.
Contents: v. 1. Afghans-Bosnians – v. 2. Brazilians-Colombians – v. 3. Colonial America-Egyptians – v. 4. Emigrés and refugees-Guyanese – v. 5. Gypsies (Romany)-Irish – v. 6. Iroquois confederacy-local politics, Canda – v. 7. Local politics, U.S.-Native Americans, Southeast – v. 8. Native Americans, Southwest and Mexico-Puerto Ricans – v. 9. Quebec separatism-social mobility and race – v. 10. South Africans-World War II.
ISBN 0-7172-5777-0 (set : alk. paper)
1. Minorities – North America – Encyclopedias, Juvenile. 2. Immigrants – North America – Encyclopedias, Juvenile. 3. Ethnology – North America – Encyclopedias, Juvenile. 4. North America – Population – Encyclopedias, Juvenile. 5. North America – History – Encyclopedias, Juvenile. 6. North America – Ethnic relations – Encyclopedias, Juvenile. [1. North America – Population – Encyclopedias. 2. Ethnology – North America – Encyclopedias.]

E49.P467 2003
305.8'0097'03 – dc21

2003042395

For information address the publisher:
Grolier, Scholastic Library Publishing,
Old Sherman Turnpike, Danbury, Connecticut 06816

Printed and bound in Singapore

For The Brown Reference Group plc
Academic Consultants: Donald Avery, Professor, Department of History, University of Western Ontario;
Margaret Connell-Szasz, Professor of Native American and Celtic History, University of New Mexico
Editors: Rachel Bean, Andrew Campbell, Dennis Cove, Felicity Crowe, Mark Fletcher, Lee Stacy
Designer: Dax Fullbrook
Picture Researcher: Becky Cox
Indexer: Kay Ollerenshaw
Managing Editor: Tim Cooke

Contents

Emigrés and refugees

Refugees and émigrés are two categories of "unwilling immigrants," that is, people who are forced to live outside their own country, and who are unable or unwilling to return due to a fear that they will be persecuted because of their race, religion, ethnicity, political affiliation, membership in a particular social group, or for any other reason. The difference between refugees and émigrés is that refugees have no interest in returning to their country, while émigrés intend to return when there is an improvement in the situation that forced them to leave.

Population statisticians can really only estimate the number of people, or groups of people, who would and could return to their home country if there were to be a change in the situation there. While an immigrant may claim that he or she would return if there were an improvement in the political or economic situation in their homeland, only time can show if this will be the case. Therefore, no actual figures are available for the number of immigrants who consider themselves émigrés rather than permanent residents of the United States. However, there are several groups known to contain large numbers of people who have not taken out U.S. citizenship, and who profess their willingness to return to their home country in the future.

Ethiopian refugees on the Kenya–Ethiopia border in 1993 wait in trucks sponsored by the United Nations High Commission for Refugees (UNHCR) to be repatriated. The refugees had fled their homeland to escape famine.

The United Nations and the Refugee

International efforts on behalf of refugees began with the Intergovernmental Agencies for Refugees (IAR), which worked under the League of Nations from 1919 to 1946. This agency was superseded by the United Nations High Commission for Refugees (UNHCR) in 1949, following the establishment of the United Nations. The commission and its predecessor oversaw the relocation of thousands of displaced persons from World War II, as well as caring for refugees from the many natural and human disasters of the 20th century. Today the UNHCR provides protection and assistance to about 27.4 million people annually, of whom 14.5 million are refugees.

Processing Refugee Applications

Within the United States refugees are processed under a special visa program based on nationality or national grouping. These refugees are sorted into four priority levels. A Priority One refugee is a person with serious concerns about their personal safety that are backed by a credible history of persecution against them. A Priority Two refugee is a person from a group of "special concern." This group currently includes certain people from Bosnia, Burma, Cuba, Iran, the former Soviet

Union, and Vietnam. Priority Three and Four refugees are those who are related to someone who qualifies as a Priority One or Two refugee, and who will therefore be permitted to immigrate under refugee asylum laws if their relation's application is granted.

In the United States the Immigration and Naturalization Service (INS) processes refugee applications. The most recent report states that in 1997, 112,741 people applied for refugee status in the United States, and 77,600 were accepted. Bosnia-Herzegovina (27,840), the former Soviet Union (27,632), Vietnam (6,522), Somalia (5,599), and Iraq (3,289) accounted for 91 percent of the applicant home countries.

Early Refugees

In the 19th century certain groups of people in Europe and Asia were forced to flee to North America. These people were persecuted for their religious beliefs, their political beliefs, or their nationality. Several thousand German fugitives from the failed liberal revolutions against the monarchy in Germany fled to the United States after 1848. In Russia from the 1880s until the 1910s a series of organized massacres of Jewish civilians forced hundreds of thousands of Jewish refugees to flee to the United States. In Turkey oppression of the Armenian people by the Turkish government resulted in over 50,000 Armenians fleeing to North America by 1914. During the 1930s many German and Austrian Jews tried to escape the racist Nazi regime in Germany. From 1935 until 1941 as many as 150,000 Jewish refugees moved to North America. After World War II many leading Spanish intellectuals sought refuge from the dictatorship of General Franco in Spain.

Emigrés in Hollywood

Hollywood—the entertainment center of the United States—is a magnet for artists, filmmakers, actors, actresses, directors, musicians, and writers who, for varying reasons, are unable to pursue their careers in their home countries. From the 1930s to the present émigrés and exiles from around the world have gone to work in Hollywood. For example, the noted film director Fritz Lang (1890–1976) fled Nazi Germany in 1933 to avoid being forced to collaborate with the Nazi government on propaganda films. He settled in the United States and went on to make such classic movies as *Ministry of Fear* (1944) and *The Big Heat* (1953).

St. Michael's Ukrainian Orthodox Church in Sandy Lake, Manitoba, Canada. For many refugee and émigré groups centers of worship become the focus of the community.

Refugee families at a United Nations' relief center in Somalia during the famine crisis of 1992. Civil war through the 1980s had contributed to the people's plight.

Eastern European Refugees

Since 1992 around 107,000 refugees from the former Yugoslavia have been admitted permanently into the United States. These refugees included Bosnian Muslims who had been detained, tortured, or experienced violence at the hands of Bosnian Serbs, and those who were liable for persecution based on their ethnic or religious identity. The INS admitted 38,654 people from the former Yugoslavia in 1999 and 20,000 in 2001.

Since 1989 more than 378,000 Jews and members of the Ukrainian Catholic or Ukrainian Orthodox churches have been admitted into the United States from the Commonwealth of Independent States (the former Soviet Union) and the Baltic states (Latvia, Lithuania, and Estonia). The INS admitted 16,922 such immigrants in 1999 and a further 17,000 in 2001.

African Refugees

Around 85,000 African refugees have been admitted permanently to the United States since 1980. This includes more than 30,000 Ethiopians, 25,000 Somalis, and smaller numbers of Sudanese, Liberians, Zaireans, Rwandans, Ugandans, Angolans, and others. In 1999 the United States admitted refugees from 24 African countries, amounting to 13,038 people accepted for permanent residence. Around 20,000 more Africans were accepted by the INS in 2001.

Many African countries have a history of economic mismanagement, political corruption, tribalism, civil wars, and harsh military dictatorships. These factors have combined to produce nations that are either unable or unwilling to support their intellectual and educated minorities. Many of these intellectuals have therefore sought emigration to the United States with the idea that they would return to their home country one day. A study from 1991 showed that 90 percent of African immigrants planned to resettle in their home countries in the future, and 67 percent of immigrants cited close family ties as an important factor in their decision to return.

Nazi Germany

From 1933 to 1945 the Nazi party of Germany forced the migration of thousands of intellectuals. In September 1933 Joseph Goebbels, the minister of propaganda, established the *Reichskulturkammer* (Reich Chamber of Culture), which oversaw the press and all types of artistic production to ensure political and aesthetic "purity." Individuals or organizations that did not conform to the Nazi ideal of Germanic culture were systematically persecuted. Thousands fled, first from Germany and then from neighboring countries that were occupied by the German military from 1939 onward. America, especially New York, became home to scientists, musicians, writers, artists, critics, publishers, actors, and many others who had been disenfranchised by the Nazis.

East Asian Refugees

Since 1975, following the end of the Vietnam War, 900,000 Vietnamese refugees have permanently settled in the United States, along with significant numbers of Highland and Lowland Lao and Khmer peoples (who are ethnic minorities in Vietnam). In total, 1.4 million Indochinese refugees have been granted asylum. In 1999 the INS approved 10,204 applications from East Asia, the majority of which were from Vietnam, with some from Burma, Laos, and other areas of Indochina. In 1999 the United States admitted 10,204 people from East Asia and took a further 10,000 refugees in 2001.

The Dalai Lama, the spiritual leader of the Tibetan people, was forced into exile in India in 1959 following 10 years of rule by the Chinese. Many Tibetans also fled into exile across the world, always hoping to return to their homeland.

West and South Asian Refugees

Since 1980 112,500 refugees from West and South Asia have been accepted into the United States permanently, including 47,000 Iranians, 31,200 Iraqis, and 28,000 Afghans. Many of these people are members of religious minorities, such as Jews, Zoroastrians, and Christians, or are from various ethnic minorities.

Many Afghans have been displaced by a combination of years of civil conflict, religious persecution, and drought. The number of refugees has been increased by the campaign against terrorism waged in Afghanistan by the United States and its allies in the wake of attacks on the World Trade Center in New York on September 11, 2001. In total, only 4,078 western and southern Asian refugees were admitted to the United States in 1999, but there were approximately 10,000 applications for asylum from the region in 2001. The figure for 2002 was expected to be higher still. Many of the Afghans admitted to the United States are doctors, scholars, and other intellectuals who fled Afghanistan during the Soviet occupation of the 1980s or, more recently, fled the hardline Taliban regime in the 1990s. Analysts have estimated that in peacetime more than 10,000 expatriates would ultimately return from the United States to help rebuild Afghanistan.

Another example of a strong émigré group is the Tibetan community. In 1949 Chinese troops invaded Tibet, which borders China, and imposed tight controls over the population. Some Tibetans fled into exile. While there are only about 3,000 Tibetans in the United States today, they are a close-knit community. They are devoted to the Dalai Lama, their spiritual leader, who formed a Tibetan government-in-exile (currently based in India). It is most likely that if Tibet were ever freed from Chinese control, many of the Tibetans now residing in the United States and elsewhere in the world would return to help rebuild their country.

Latin American and Caribbean Refugees

The State Department of the United States considers voluntary repatriation the most durable solution for the refugee problem in Latin America and the Caribbean. The INS maintains an "unallocated reserve" of 4,000 immigration places to allow for refugees from a

Useful websites

U.S. Cultural Orientation Resource Center (www.cal.org/rsc/cubans/IMMI.HTM)
The U.S Immigration and Naturalization Service (www.ins.usdoj.gov/graphics/glossary3.htm#R)
U.S. Committee for Refugees (www.refugees.org/)
Tibet Online (www.tibet.org/)
United Nations High Commission for Refugees (www.unhcr.ch/cgi-bin/texis/vtx/home)

Hundreds of Cuban refugees crowd around a makeshift immigration center on the dockside in Miami, Florida, having made the trip by boat from Cuba. Florida has an extensive community of Cuban exiles who have escaped the economic hardships of their homeland.

variety of countries and regions not otherwise provided for in their allocation plans. This policy allows for the approval of some refugee applications from people of Latin American and Caribbean origin, should circumstances warrant it. However, no specific statistics on annual entries permitted on this basis are available for the region.

The most significant number of refugees from the Caribbean to the United States come from Cuba. The majority of Cuban refugees are former political prisoners, forced labor conscripts, human rights activists, and people who have been persecuted for their religious beliefs. The United States admitted approximately 3,200 Cubans in 2001, but the INS also accepted approximately 17,000 Cuban admissions through other legal means of immigration.

The Cubans are a unique émigré story in the history of the United States. Given Cuba's close geographical proximity, it is not a surprise that many Cubans have moved to North America. Since 1959 more than a million Cubans have left their homeland to escape the communist regime of Fidel Castro. A vital factor in the legal and illegal immigration of Cubans into the United States is the official assumption that anyone from Cuba is automatically a refugee, so Cubans do not have to prove that they are fleeing from political persecution to gain refugee status.

Overall, the number of émigrés and refugees currently living in North America cannot be tallied accurately, but the United States accepted a total of 85,006 refugees in 1999, the most recent statistics available. Given the present status of the refugee question worldwide, as well as ongoing wars and conflicts around the globe, it is likely that refugees will continue to be admitted into the United States for many years to come.

See also

- Afghans (Volume 1)
- African Americans (Volume 1)
- Cubans (Volume 3)
- Immigration and Naturalization Service (Volume 5)
- Jews (Volume 6)
- Vietnamese (Volume 10)

English

One 20th-century American author, Charlotte Erickson, characterized the English in America as the "invisible immigrants" largely due to the fact that they have always integrated easily into American society and culture. That is because in large measure the earliest immigrants to North America were English and Scottish, and the society they founded had its roots in the British Isles of the 17th century. From this early colonial period onward newly arriving English immigrants were immersed in a culture that largely had the same language, political structures, religions, and social hierarchies as their homeland. Even though several notable differences subsequently emerged—the widespread republicanization of institutions, wider suffrage, and the absence of an established nationalized church—more than most other ethnic groups, the English enjoyed higher acceptance in their new homeland and assimilated more quickly. To varying degrees this has always been the case with English immigrants to North America.

Who are the English?

The meaning of the term "English" is often ambiguous. England itself is the largest and southernmost of the three countries that make up what is now Great Britain, bordering Scotland to the north and Wales to the west. Inhabited since prehistoric times, England has rarely been an easily classifiable nation. It had a succession of invaders and rulers—including Romans, Anglo-Saxons, Vikings, and Normans—before becoming united with Wales in the mid-16th century and with Scotland in 1707. Although the Scots and Welsh have their own distinct traditions, many aspects of "Englishness" are shared by all of Britain's peoples. In this article the term "English" is used to describe not only people and culture from England itself, but also some aspects of culture that are common throughout Great Britain.

The English in Colonial America

The English were the first Europeans to settle along the eastern coast of what became the United States. They established the first permanent settlement in Jamestown, Virginia, in 1607, followed by the Plymouth and Massachusetts Bay colonies between 1620 and 1622. Pilgrim settlements attracted 20,000 immigrants between 1620 and 1642. However, many English settlers ultimately made their homes in New Hampshire, Maine, Rhode Island, and Connecticut. Many of these

A replica of the flagship Susan Constant, *one of three vessels that brought the first English settlers to America in 1607. The 105 men and boys aboard founded the first permanent North American colony in Jamestown, Virginia.*

Fact File: ENGLISH

Distribution

English Americans live in every U.S. state and major city.

Most populous states:
- California
- Texas
- Florida
- New York
- Ohio

Most populous cities:
- New York City
- Los Angeles
- San Francisco
- Dallas
- Houston

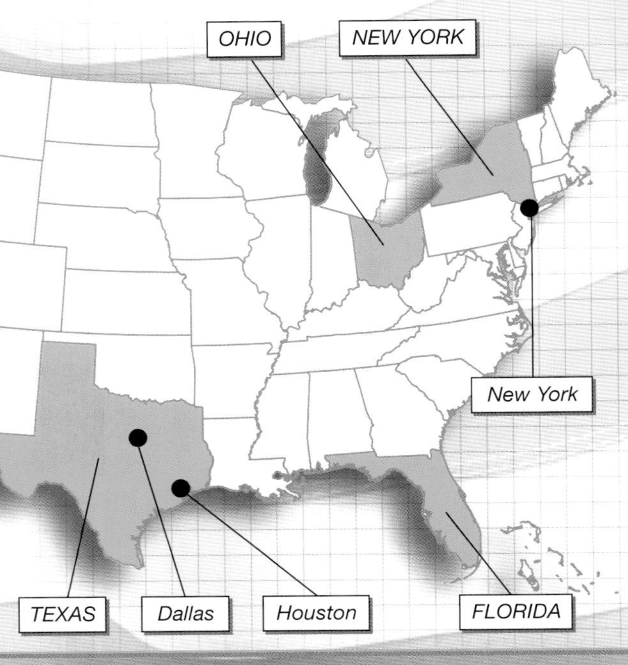

Region of origin

England

England is in the United Kingdom (Great Britain).

Population

The 2000 U.S. census shows 19,152,663 people as being "of English descent."

Language

English. It is the primary language of the United States.

Names

Common English surnames include Smith, Taylor, Brown, Wilson, Thomas, and Johnson.

Dates of major arrivals

1628–1642; 1720s; 1750s; 1760–1780; 1825–1840; 1845–1847; 1864–1873; 1882–1893; 1940s; and 1960s.

First immigrants

The earliest English immigrants to the New World arrived in 1607 and founded the first permanent North American colony in Jamestown, Virginia.

Useful websites

Modern British surnames (http://homepages.newnet.co.uk/dance/webpjd/index.htm)
Trans-Atlantic Brides and Parents Association (www.geocities.com/tbpabritish2/4U.html)
Angela Lansbury Biography (www.sharf.com/jennie/lansbury/bio.htm)
British music (www.travelbritain.com/SocietyandCulture/BritishMusic.html)
The Society of Friends (www.quaker.org)
Guy Fawkes Day—background and history of the English holiday (www.ueharlax.ac.uk/campus/sao/Spec_Events/GFD.htm)
British Expatriate Network (www.british-expats.com)
The British community in America (www.britishinamerica.com)

Religion

Many English immigrants belong to the Anglican Church of England, and tend to become members of the Episcopal, Methodist, or Baptist churches in the United States because the denominations are similar. Some English immigrants are members of the Catholic Church and continue to practice their faith in the United States. No statistics are available on the number of adherents to any particular denomination among immigrants from England or English Americans.

Festivals

St. George's Day (April 23) celebrates the patron saint of England. Some communities celebrate Guy Fawkes Day (November 5).

Food

English dishes include fish and chips, roast beef and Yorkshire pudding, Cornish pasties, and spotted dick (a pudding).

new settlements were established by religious reformers who had not been accepted in Massachusetts. A significant event in English domination of the region came in 1664, when the Royal Navy captured the Dutch trading post of New Amsterdam and renamed it New York.

Immigration from England to colonial America averaged several thousand annually from the late 1620s to 1700. The new immigrants from England came from nearly every background, but the majority were working-class families and indentured servants (people bound to work for a master or mistress for a set period, often in return for their passage to America). The Chesapeake Bay area of Virginia was settled by a small number of gentry, clergy, lawyers, officials, and even some minor aristocracy. By the 1690s the English and their descendants made up 90 percent of the European settlers in colonial America. From 1720 until the American Revolution in 1775–1783 English immigration fluctuated depending on the economic and political situation in England and the colonies. Between 1717 and 1776, 30,000 male and female prisoners convicted of serious felonies were transported to Virginia and Maryland, as well as Pennsylvania—a colony originally established by the Englishman William Penn in 1682 as a "tolerance settlement" for Quakers.

William Penn (1644–1718), founder of Pennsylvania, making a treaty with local Native Americans in 1682. An immigrant from London, England, Penn established elective government in his colonies and built the city of Philadelphia.

By 1763 all of the 13 colonies had come under the control of the British government, which imposed the English language, English laws, governmental administration, education, commercial and financial management, and English culture in general on its new possessions. While the American Revolution changed this situation, the broad influence of English culture remained. According to the census of 1790, the English constituted 60 percent of European settlers in North America and half of the four million colonists.

Declining Immigration

Though largely seen as "invisible immigrants," a series of conflicts—chiefly the American Revolution and the subsequent 1812–1815 war between the United States and Britain—led to division between English settlers and naturalized Americans. Immigration to the American colonies from England fell sharply between 1780 and 1815. Several thousand English Loyalists were forced to leave after 1783, many moving northward to Canada, thus strengthening English influence in Canadian society. During the 1812–1815 war many English immigrants in the former colonies were considered

American volunteers marching against the British during the American Revolution (1775–1883). The war caused a steep decline in emigration from England to North America.

potential enemies and were subject to prejudicial laws and, in some cases, internment or enforced separation from the rest of the population. The English were ordered to register with the local magistrate, and some 10,000 did. Some English secured waivers from registration or internment because they owned property, were married to an American citizen, or had declared their intention to become naturalized Americans before the war started. In general the prejudice lasted only until the end of the war in 1815. On the English side immigration dropped, partly due to British involvement in India and Latin America, which attracted some English settlers. A further factor was the period of warfare in Europe. Soldiers were needed to protect the British Isles, and so fewer English were permitted to emigrate to North America.

Throughout the 19th century immigrants from England continued to come to the United States, although their numbers were low and steady compared with those from other parts of Europe and the Mediterranean. However, annual English immigration increased to more than 60,000 in the late 1860s and continued to rise until 1872, when it peaked at 75,000. The final and most consistent wave of immigration from England lasted from 1872 to 1893. The immigrants were drawn by the completion of the transcontinental railroad, which helped open the West to settlement, as well as by the cheaper steamship passage fares that allowed them to cross the Atlantic. Immigrants in the early part of the 19th century tended to travel with one or more family members, and craftsmen outnumbered farmers three to one. By the end of the century both unskilled and semiskilled laborers, miners, and building trade workers constituted the bulk of English immigrants. The ability of these immigrants to transfer their skills to the rapidly industrialization taking place in North America ensured their successful assimilation in their new homeland.

English war brides

Many American servicemen were stationed in England during World War II. During their time in England tens of thousands of American soldiers met and married English women. These English brides often returned to the United States with their husbands or arrived in the United States soon after. Some joined groups like the Washington GI Brides Club (below), which helped introduce them to U.S. culture and society. Today, associations like the Trans-Atlantic Brides and Parents Association (TBPA) work to keep these brides, their descendants, and their families close to each other. Local TBPA groups meet for social events like the November 5 Guy Fawkes bonfire or for soccer or darts matches.

20th-Century Immigration

English immigration remained steady during the first four decades of the 20th century despite the favorable allowance shown to the English in the 1920s quota system. However, during the 1940s the number of immigrants increased to more than 100,000. This wave of immigration differed from earlier ones in that there were four women for every man who immigrated—many were war brides arriving between 1945 and 1948. Overall,

English immigrants accounted for about 12 percent of Europeans immigrating into the United States throughout the 20th century, with a notable increase in the 1960s, when they comprised 15.5 percent.

From 1957 to 1964 more physicians and surgeons emigrated from England than from any other country. The English contribution to professional occupations within North America, commonly referred to in England as the "brain drain," continues to this day. In 1974 and 1975 professional and technical workers made up over half of all English immigrants to the United States. Almost 40 percent of English immigrants in the 1970s settled in the states of Massachusetts, California, or New York, where their special skills were needed in, for example, finance, commerce, and the blossoming computer industry.

English American actors

English actors and actresses who have made a name for themselves in the United States, and in some cases become American citizens, include: Julie Andrews, Helena Bonham Carter, Charlie Chaplin, Judi Dench, Minnie Driver, Ralph Fiennes, Cary Grant, Hugh Grant, Alec Guiness, Rex Harrison, Bob Hope, Elizabeth Hurley, Stan Laurel, Ian McKellen, Dudley Moore, Gary Oldman, Vanessa Redgrave, Jean Simmons, Elizabeth Taylor, and Emma Thompson.

English Americans and Assimilation

Assimilation into American culture has often been smooth for English immigrants and their children. English Americans and Americans of English descent have been less likely to consider themselves as a minority or to feel their "Englishness" as a source of particular ethnic pride. Unlike many African, Hispanic, or Asian Americans, and other minorities, the English tendency to intermarry with other nationalities and to move from place to place makes it difficult to describe them as a distinct ethnic group. For example, one study concluded that in 1900 fewer than 20 percent of children of English parentage married someone of English descent. The high assimilation rate makes it difficult to trace English immigrants beyond the first generation.

Another important factor is that many English immigrants did not travel directly from England to the United States. Many people of English descent have arrived in America from Canada, as well as from other member nations of the British Commonwealth, such as Australia, New Zealand, and South Africa. Canadian immigrants were not accurately counted in the 19th century, and Canadians of English ancestry were not differentiated from those of Irish or French descent. These factors make the English immigrant to America difficult to trace historically and hard to quantify in modern times.

Arts and Culture

The history of American arts and culture is inextricably bound to that of English theater, literature, and in modern times, film. English colonial Americans prided themselves that America was "England outside England." They invited English actors and entertainers to the colonies to perform, and English political writers and novelists were popular. Today the entertainment

Opening night at the Shakespeare Festival in Central Park, New York. English culture in the form of theater, literature, popular music, and the arts permeates North American society.

Crew races on the Charles River at Harvard University, Cambridge, Massachusetts. Founded in 1636, Harvard is the oldest educational institution in North America and was modeled on its older counterpart in Cambridge, England.

industry is still full of English Americans, and English people who either choose to live in the United States or commute for work reasons from Britain. From the beginning of the film industry to the Broadway of today these actors, actresses, directors, and artists of all kinds have contributed to the vibrancy of American entertainment.

It is often impossible to discern where English and American cultures divide. English history is woven so tightly into the fabric of American culture it is sometimes difficult to remember that Robin Hood and King Arthur are English rather than American legends. Other examples of this "crossover culture" include the Shakespeare festivals held annually in North America. Memorable characters from English literature such as A.A. Milne's Winnie the Pooh, Lewis Carroll's Alice, and Sir Arthur Conan Doyle's Sherlock Holmes are household names in America. Writers such as J.R.R. Tolkien, author of *The Lord of the Rings*, and Ian Fleming who wrote the James Bond novels, are popular. Even Andy Capp, a comic-strip antihero of the English working class, is syndicated in American newspapers.

English Pop Music

In terms of popular music English bands and performers are widely known in the United States and Canada. After the "invasion"of North America by the English pop group the Beatles in 1964, musicians such as Eric Clapton, Elvis Costello, Peter Gabriel, and Elton John continue to enjoy huge sales in the United States, and English groups such as the Rolling Stones and Pink Floyd attract massive audiences whenever they perform in America. Overall, English and American musicians and groups appear to enjoy a symbiotic relationship in influence and artistic endeavor.

Stan Laurel

Stan Laurel (1890–1965) was born Arthur Stanley Jefferson in Ulverston, England. He had a vaudeville background, emigrating to America in 1913 while traveling with one of Fred Karno's entertainment groups, which also included Charlie Chaplin. He made a series of movies for Universal Pictures before teaming up with Oliver Hardy in 1927 to become part of the most successful comedy duo in cinema history. Together, Laurel and Hardy made 117 films between 1927 and 1952, and they received an Academy Award in 1932 for their short film *The Music Box*.

Sports and Education

English immigrants have left an indelible impression on the sports of America. The more aristocratic pursuits of lawn tennis, horse racing, and sailing have become billion-dollar businesses in the United States and enjoy ardent fan support. American universities still have sculling (rowing) and rugby teams for interuniversity competition or for recreation. The popular sport of football is an adaptation of the English game of rugby. Americans also enjoy watching and participating in English football (soccer) and support a men's and a women's national team; the men's team reached the quarter finals of the 2002 World Cup. All of these sports derive directly from English pastimes.

English immigrants were among the earliest and most fervent supporters of education in the United States. The establishment of free public schools was an important priority of both the Puritans and the English Quakers. Other English settlers favored private colleges and universities affiliated to their religious denominations. For example, in 1636 Reverend John Harvard, born in England, left £780 and 400 books to establish a college in Cambridge, Massachusetts, to train ministers: Harvard University, founded in that year, is the realization of his dream. In the 20th century the English commitment to education continues in the form of various exchange scholarships, such as the Rhodes Scholarship (1902) and Commonwealth Scholarship (1925). These student exchanges have strengthened bonds among the academic, business, and political circles of both the United States and England.

Politics and the Home Country

The predominance of English immigrants in the colonial period has had a profound effect on the United States. The country maintains English as its official language, it has an English-style court system, and Congress has two houses, much like the English Parliament. In early times a significant number of English laws became part of U.S. legal codes. There was for a long time a popular admiration for "things English," especially in U.S. cities. In New England and some Southern states in particular there was a desire to emulate English culture and lifestyles.

On a broader scale the British–American alliance, begun in World War I, continues today. The alliance allows British immigrants to maintain strong, nonconflicting political associations with their home country. The ongoing support of the United Kingdom for American undertakings was shown in 1991 by Conservative Prime Minister John Major's support for the Persian Gulf War against Iraq and again by Labour Prime Minister Tony Blair's support for the War against Terrorism, which began following the destruction of the World Trade Center in New York City on September 11, 2001.

Angela Lansbury

Born in London, England, in 1925, Angela Lansbury moved to America in 1940, becoming a U.S. citizen in 1951. She is well known for her roles in such films as *Gaslight* (1944), for which she received an Oscar nomination, *The Manchurian Candidate* (1963), *Bedknobs and Broomsticks* (1972), and *Death on the Nile* (1978). Her Broadway stage work includes several notable musicals, such as *Gypsy* (1974) and *Sweeney Todd* (1979). For 12 seasons Angela Lansbury played Jessica Fletcher in the TV mystery series *Murder, She Wrote* (1984–1996). In 1991 she provided the voice for the housekeeper-teapot in Disney's animated musical film *Beauty and the Beast*.

See also

- Canadians, English (Volume 2)
- Colonial America (Volume 3)
- Education (Volume 3)
- Scots (Volume 9)
- Welsh (Volume 10)

Estonians

Cultural organizations

Estonians in North America have worked hard to maintain ties to their culture and language. Many organizations were created to help new immigrants and to hold cultural activities throughout North America. Through the Estonian-American National Council 14 schools were established to teach the Estonian language. Many other clubs and social organizations have also been established.

See also

- Latvians (Volume 6)
- Lithuanians (Volume 6)
- Russians (Volume 9)

Estonia, once part of the Soviet Union, is a small country located on the east coast of the Baltic Sea. The current population of Estonia is 1.6 million, with 65 percent of the people having Estonian origin, and 30 percent having Russian ancestry.

Immigration to North America occurred in two waves. The first wave took place in the early 1900s, as Estonians emigrated to find jobs, mostly in labor, industry, and construction. Major settlements in the United States during this period were located in New York, San Francisco, and Fort Pierre, South Dakota. Early Estonian immigrants to the United States were officially classified as Russian.

The second wave took place during World War II (1939–1945), when people fled German and later Soviet occupation. Between 1940 and 1944 almost 10 percent of the Estonian population left Estonia for other countries, such as nearby Sweden. Of these emigrants about 20,000 went to North America, mainly to larger cities like Toronto, New York, and San Francisco. Today Ontario has the largest Estonian population in the world outside Estonia (15,440 according to the 1996 census). Most of these new immigrants were well educated and quickly became part of the middle class. They included musicians, artists, and writers, as well as engineers and other professionals.

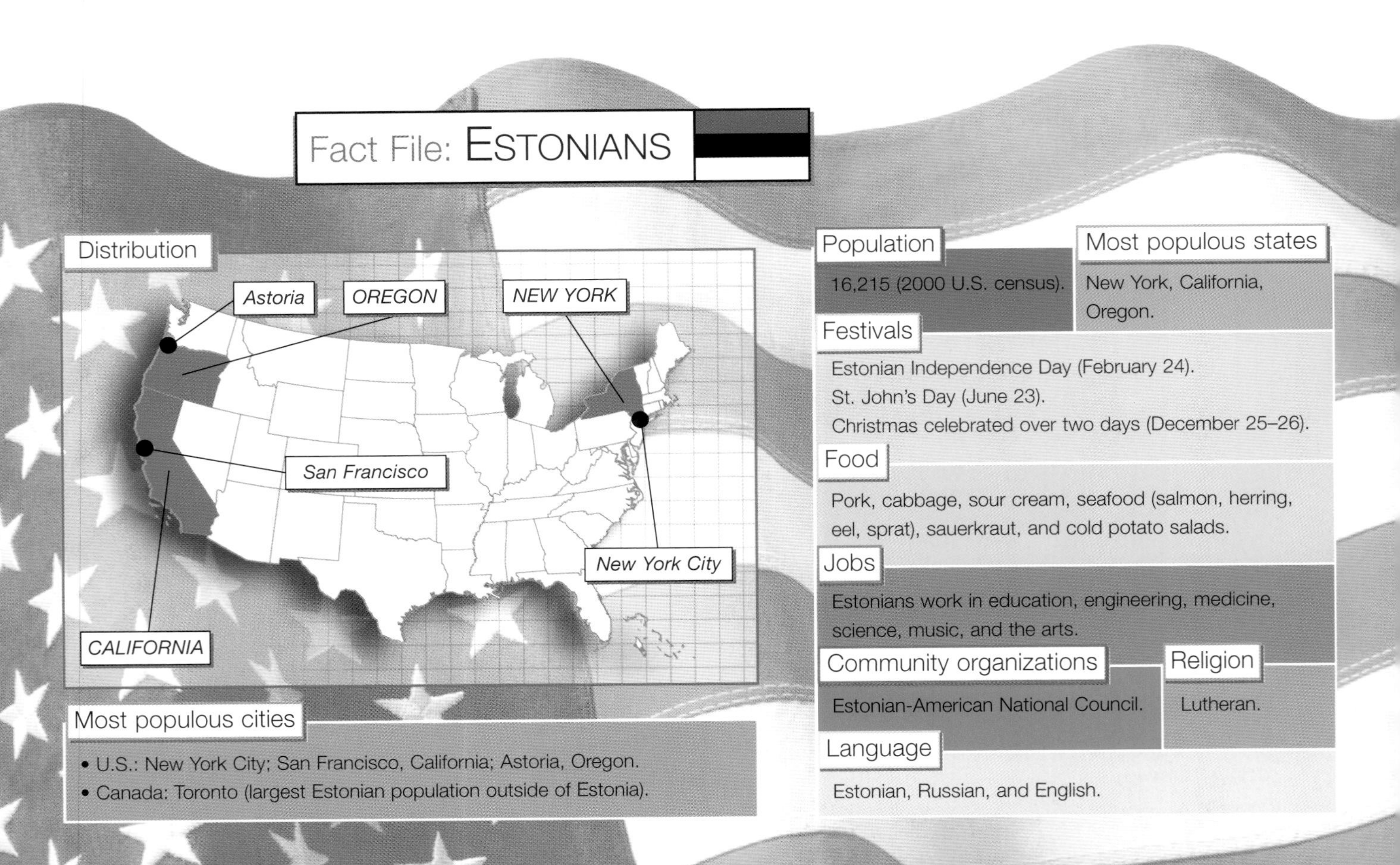

Ethiopians

The Republic of Ethiopia is the 10th largest country in Africa and lies in the northeast of the continent, bordered by Eritrea, Djibouti, Somalia, Kenya, and Sudan. Subsistence agriculture is the economic staple, although droughts have diminished crops in recent years. Some 85 percent of the population lives in rural areas.

The country has been marked by political instability. In the early 1930s Haile Selassie became emperor of Ethiopia. His rule was interrupted when Italian troops occupied the country from 1935 to 1941, and he was deposed in a military coup in 1974. The succeeding presidency of Colonel Mengistu lasted until he was forced into exile in 1991. Tigréan guerrillas then seized the capital city, Addis Ababa, and established a temporary government. Ethiopia was also in conflict with Eritrea after trying to annex the country in 1962. Eritrea recovered its independence in 1993. A border war with Ethiopia that erupted in 1998 ended under United Nations auspices in 2000.

Against this backdrop of political instability and widespread famine large numbers of Ethiopians have migrated to major U.S. cities such as Boston, New York, and Washington, D.C. Of Africans emigrating to the United States today, the Ethiopians are second in number only to Nigerians. Education is important to many Ethiopian families, and Ethiopian attendance at U.S. universities is high.

Useful websites

Ethiopia News Site (http://news.newmalaysia.com/world/africa/ethiopia.shtml)

The Murulle Foundation based in Colorado is a charity committed to conserving the balance between cultural and natural resources in sub-Saharan Africa, beginning with projects in Ethiopia (www.murulle.org/)

See also

- African Americans (Volume 1)
- African Canadians (Volume 1)
- Central Africans (Volume 2)
- East Africans (Volume 3)
- Education (Volume 3)
- Egyptians (Volume 3)

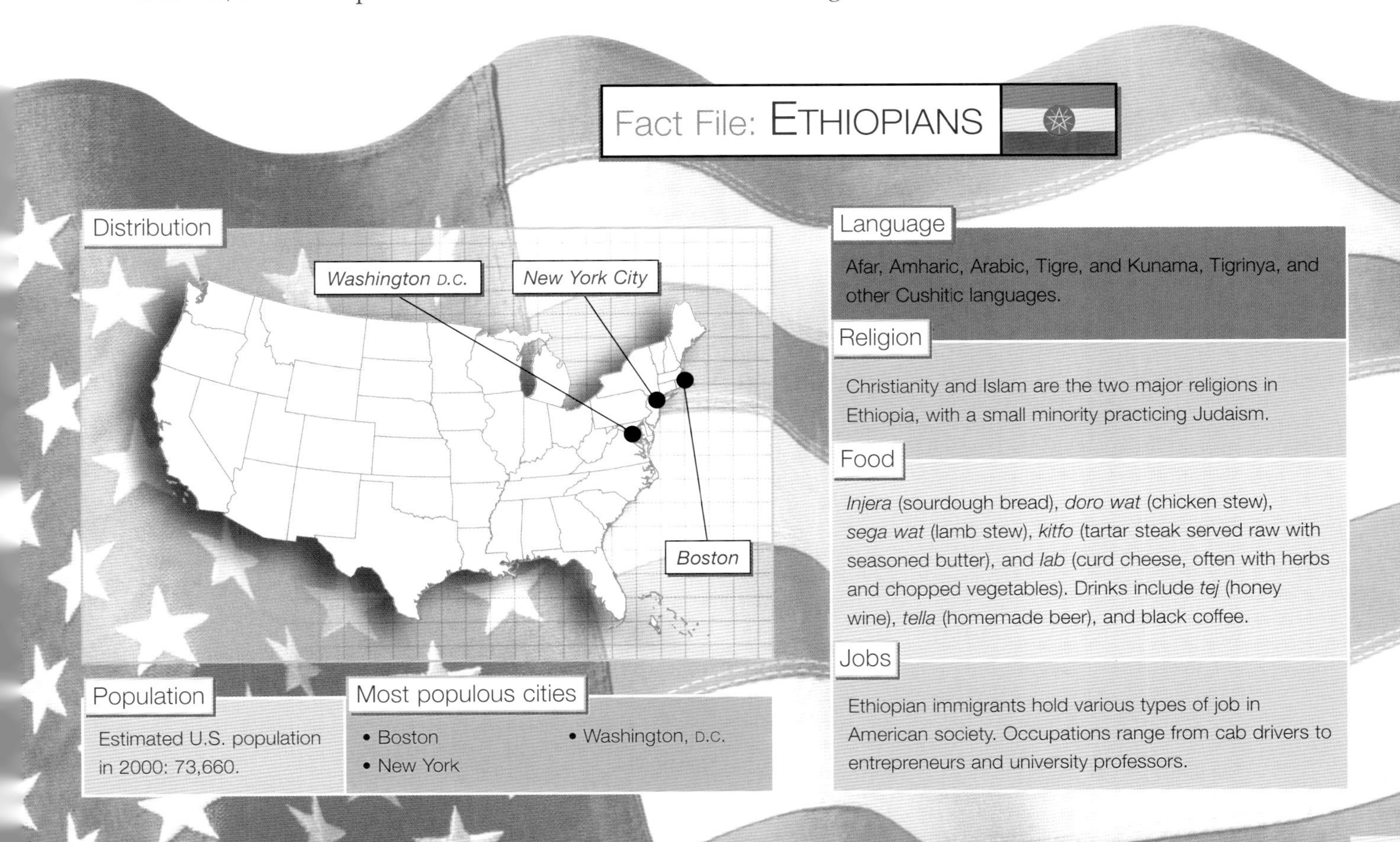

Fact File: ETHIOPIANS

Distribution

Language

Afar, Amharic, Arabic, Tigre, and Kunama, Tigrinya, and other Cushitic languages.

Religion

Christianity and Islam are the two major religions in Ethiopia, with a small minority practicing Judaism.

Food

Injera (sourdough bread), *doro wat* (chicken stew), *sega wat* (lamb stew), *kitfo* (tartar steak served raw with seasoned butter), and *lab* (curd cheese, often with herbs and chopped vegetables). Drinks include *tej* (honey wine), *tella* (homemade beer), and black coffee.

Jobs

Ethiopian immigrants hold various types of job in American society. Occupations range from cab drivers to entrepreneurs and university professors.

Population

Estimated U.S. population in 2000: 73,660.

Most populous cities

- Boston
- New York
- Washington, D.C.

Family patterns

Many Americans believe that the family is the foundation of society. The family preserves traditions and is idealized as the "nuclear" family unit, consisting of parents and their children. Ethnic European peoples migrating to the United States have brought family patterns that have served to either alter or support that basic American view of family life. In addition, indigenous Native Americans, African Americans, Hispanics, and Asian Americans have introduced, preserved, and adapted their own family patterns.

Changes in family patterns among ethnic groups are complex and can vary with successive waves of immigrants from the same homeland. For example, established immigrants and the first-generation of their descendants, who have adopted American family patterns, are reminded of their native customs by the arrival of new immigrants. For many immigrants family life, based on ties of affection, obligation, and tradition, has been their closest link to their homeland and ethnic identity. Today family structures and relationships among native-born citizens, older immigrants, and newer immigrants display a variety of patterns. In 2000 the average size of foreign-born households was 3.26 persons. This figure was larger than the average established American household, which was 2.54 persons. Among European immigrants the household average was 2.38 people, compared to an average of 3.18 people among Asian immigrants and 3.72 among Latin American immigrants.

The American family today

The traditional "nuclear" family has a working father, a housewife mother, and two children. In reality such a family structure accounts for only 7 percent of American households today. Families in which both parents work and families with dual incomes and no children heavily outnumber the traditional model. An increasing number of families are headed by single parents, either male or female.

Types of European Immigrant

New European immigrants came to America in three basic family types: first, the complete (or nearly complete) family; second, married immigrants or couples; and third, the individual immigrant (unmarried with no children). Migration to North America always contained a mixture of these three groups. Also, these groups could and did mix randomly after immigration, and changes in their status often occurred.

History shows a constant mixture of types of immigrant. In the 17th century the English Puritans who emigrated to New England consisted mainly of families. Young, unmarried Englishmen largely settled the Chesapeake Bay and Middle Colonies. By the early 19th century young, unmarried men generally outnumbered the migrating family groups among the English, Scots, Welsh, Irish, and Germans, but family migration was still common. Between 1840 and 1850 the rapid rise of industrialization and urbanization in North America attracted young, single men to immigrate, as they saw opportunities for employment in the new industrial plants and factories that were springing up. By the late 1800s immigration from southern and eastern Europe brought more unmarried males and some more family groups.

An Italian immigrant family arriving at Ellis Island, New York, in 1905. Families and increasing numbers of single men left countries like Italy to escape poverty and find work in the industrial plants and factories that flourished in American cities from the 19th century onward.

In the late 19th century many single men immigrated and joined—or were helped by—extended family members who had previously immigrated. Many of these young, single men and women came to work in the United States temporarily and planned to return home. Table 1 (below) shows statistics for the percentages of immigrants to the United States who returned to their homeland between 1910 and 1914. It shows that one in five Hungarian (Magyar) and Slovak immigrants returned home within 30 months, but fewer than one in 40 of the Jews and Czechs returned to Europe to live. The table also provides figures on immigrant gender. In every group the number of male immigrants was higher than female immigrants. In addition, in some groups like the Greeks, the men outnumbered the women 11 to 1. This fact in itself made the continuation of a Greek lifestyle and culture in North America very difficult because Greek men were unlikely to find Greek women to marry. The ratio of three men to one woman among southern Italians and nearly two men to one woman among

Group	Males	Females	Number of males to 1,000 females
Czechs	5%	10%	1,329
English	6%	13%	1,358
Finnish	7%	15%	1,812
Germans	7%	16%	1,318
Greeks	16%	12%	11,696
Hungarians (Magyars)	22%	38%	1,406
Italians (South)	17%	15%	3,200
Jews	2%	3%	1,172
Poles	13%	16%	1,876
Slovaks	19%	27%	1,622

Table 1. This table shows the percentage of immigrant groups in the United States who returned to their homeland between 1910 and 1914. Figures in the right-hand column show the number of male to female immigrants in each immigrant community. (Compiled by Ameristat based on statistics from the U.S. Census Bureau.)

A traditional Jewish wedding ceremony in Brooklyn, New York, in 1971. Jewish cultural traditions and the prejudice of other communities have meant there has often been less intermarriage between Jews and other cultural groups than there has been between many other communities.

Finns and Poles also was more likely to lead to a high proportion of intercultural marriages in these groups.

European Ethnic Family Patterns

Among married men who immigrated alone there appear to have been two outcomes. Stories of forgotten wives were common, but so were stories of marriages that were undermined by a period of separation, but which, when the couples were reunited, were restored to their traditional foundation. Most unmarried men found wives in North America. According to figures shown in Table 2 (below), most took brides from their ethnic community, while a few (such as the English) married largely outside their own group. Availability of same-culture partners and the openness of cultures to partners from different ethnic groups were shaping factors. Both first- and second-generation Englishmen, for example, appear to have been open to marriages with non-English partners. However, among some groups, such as the Jews, religion and prejudice played pivotal roles. Jewish culture encourages marriage to Jewish partners, and because of anti-Semitism Jews often found it difficult to intermarry with other cultural groups.

The development and promotion of ethnic family patterns was often linked to the age of marriage, the type of family formation, and the number of children common within the ethnic group. For example, a substantial number of Italian and Polish immigrant women married in their teens, whereas English, Irish, and second-generation American women tended to marry later. A comparison of Irish and Italian women reveals that in the first generation Irish women married, on average, five years later than Italian women. In the second generation the difference was only two years. Census data also indicate that immigrants generally had more children than native-born Americans, but the number of children varies. Rural

Table 2. This table shows the percentage of marriages outside ethnic groups in first- and second-generation immigrant communities in New York City in the years 1908 to 1912.

Group	First generation (immigrant)	Second generation (native born)
English	61%	82%
Germans	20%	26%
Irish	10%	30%
Jews	1%	6%
Poles	9%	17%

families were often larger than urban ones. This difference may be due to lower fertility rates or to the living conditions in urban America, which fostered disease and high child mortality among first-generation immigrants.

A group of Slavic immigrants boarding with a family in New York City in 1912. New immigrants often lived with other families until they could afford their own homes.

Household Structure

Ethnic groups commonly organized their households along the same lines as native-born Americans, as independent "nuclear" families consisting of two parents and their children. In times of temporary stress, such as increased immigration, housing shortages, or economic downturns, households sometimes also included relatives. Historical census data indicates that only rarely did more than 10 to 15 percent of American households contain extended family relations. If a relative moved in to live with a nuclear family, it was likely to be an aging parent or a newlywed couple living with parents.

In opposition to their American counterparts, ethnic families were more likely to take in nonrelative borders as "guests" or "subtenants." This provided additional income for the family. Typically, boarders were young men or women who were in the stage between leaving their parents and getting married. Often, ethnic families also became "guests" or "subtenants" in other people's homes. The frequency of such housing arrangements decreased the longer the person or family stayed in the United States.

One particular type of extended family was and is especially problematic in North America. In most of the Muslim world and among a small number of other ethnic or religious groups, such as the Mormons, the practice of polygamy, or having more than one wife, was once common, and it is still followed in the 21st century, though the practice is not as widespread as in the past. Polygamy was outlawed by the U.S. Congress in the 1860s, and it remains illegal in the United States and Canada. It is also considered to be morally unacceptable by an overwhelming majority of North Americans.

Immigrant settlement

Almost a million new immigrants a year make the United States their home. Rather than settling evenly across the nation, over 65 percent have stayed in just 10 cities. They probably settle here for two reasons. First, U.S. immigration law strongly favors family reunification, and second, cities offer social and economic support networks to new immigrants.

Hispanic Families

Two of the largest groups of Hispanic peoples in North America are Mexicans and Cubans. There are large Mexican American communities in California, New Mexico, and Texas. For Mexican Americans the family plays a key role in providing stability and a sense of support, especially as many Mexicans in the United States have to face a lack of social and political support. The family structure

A Finnish American family from Minnesota singing traditional Finnish Christmas carols. Songs, music, dance, and cooking are some of the cultural expressions through which families keep their cultural heritage alive.

often extends to include neighbors and friends. It is usually led by the father, who makes the decisions, and there is a rigid hierarchy based on age and gender. Mexican American families tend to be larger than average U.S. families. According to the 2000 U.S. census, 33.1 percent of Mexican households consist of more than five people. Although males are still the family heads in the majority of cases, single-parent families run by the mother have increased to 21.1 percent of all Mexican American families.

After Fidel Castro took control of Cuba following the Cuban Revolution in 1959, hundreds of thousands of Cubans immigrated to the United States, to Florida and Miami in particular. Like other Hispanics, Cuban Americans view the family as an important structure for giving stability and strength. Cuban Americans born in Cuba have larger families than Cuban Americans born in the United States, which is probably a reflection of more conservative values among the Catholic Cuban-born parents.

Asian Families

A long history of discrimination against Asians in the United States meant that few Chinese, Japanese, or Filipinos married white Americans before the 1960s. The Chinese first began immigrating in significant numbers during the Gold Rush of 1848. Most were men who came to work as miners or laborers. In 1852 there were only seven Chinese women among 11,794 Chinese men. New Chinese arrivals were linked through "family associations"—organizations of individuals with the same surname, or family name. During the late 19th century the Chinese faced a series of discriminatory laws that prevented them from being assimilated into U.S. society. Today there is more intermarriage between Chinese and non-Chinese. However, many Chinese Americans continue to embrace traditional family structures, encouraging their adult children to remain at home until they get married so that they can contribute to the family wealth.

The majority of first-generation Japanese arrived in California between 1891 and 1924. They came in search of work in factories and mines, on the railroads, and on farms. As a result of Californian legislation in the first half of the 20th century preventing Japanese from marrying whites, Japanese usually married within their ethnic

Office of Minority Health

This U.S. government department focuses on public health issues affecting Native Americans, Alaska Natives, Asian Americans, Native Hawaiians and other Pacific Islanders, African Americans, and Hispanics. It is working to improve the health of ethnic populations through the development of effective health policies and programs that take into account the specific cultural characteristics of the group. For more information see the Office of Minority Health website (www.omhrc.gov).

group. Since the 1960s, when legislation was changed, about half of all Japanese Americans have married partners from outside their group.

Filipino men came to the United States at the start of the 20th century either for education or for work. From 1913 to the 1930s the ratio of Filipino men to Filipino women was 14 to 1, so most of the men were unable to find Filipino wives. At the same time, California law prevented Asian immigrants (defined as "Mongolians") from marrying white women. As a result, many Filipino men intermarried with Mexican and Puerto Rican women.

Interracial parents with their children in New York City. Marriage between different ethnic groups continues to be an important aspect of American society.

African American Families

Most Africans were brought to the United States and Canada as slaves. Slavery and poverty did much to erode the strength of the African American family as husbands and wives were often forcibly separated and children taken from parents. At the start of the 20th century many African American families moved from the south of the United States to the north in search of work in the major cities. In urban environments it was common for men to work as laborers and for their wives to work outside the home as cooks or domestics. African American households had relatively low levels of income, and poverty is one of the factors that has contributed to the breakdown of family structures. In the late 1990s nearly 50 percent of African American children lived in single-parent families with their mothers.

Native American Families

During the 1800s intermarriage between women from certain Native American peoples, such as the Cherokee and the Creek, and whites was not uncommon. However, traditional Native American families were very different from the typical European family unit. Most Native American families were matrilineal, which means that the family was based around the wife's extended family of grandmother, married daughters, their spouses, and children. To avoid family conflict the Apache people had a custom that forbade a mother-in-law from talking to her son-in-law, however it was permissable for a grandmother to talk to her granddaughter's husband.

Extended family ties are still very strong in Native American communities. Today in North America although many Navajo have moved away to live and work in cities, they continue to send money home to their families living on reservations.

Useful websites

The Vital Records of the United States give information on birth, death, marriage, and divorce in the United States (www.vitalrec.com)

The FedStats homepage gives access to over 100 Federal agencies (www.fedstats.gov)

Other useful websites include:

U.S. population data (www.ameristat.org)

U.S. Census Bureau Home Page (www.census.gov)

U.S. Immigration and Naturalization Service (www.ins.gov)

See also

- Assimilation (Volume 1)
- Cultural mingling (Volume 3)
- Cultural retention (Volume 3)
- Returnees (Volume 9)
- Segregation and integration (Volume 9)

Festivals

Festivals are times of celebration that provide a welcome change from everyday life. In North America they range in size from small homegrown events to large-scale celebrations designed to attract thousands of people. Ethnic, religious, and other community groups organize these events to publicly display and reaffirm important aspects of their culture or history. The ceremonial nature of festivals underscores their traditional roots, with accompanying pageantry that nearly always includes special music, dance, food and drink, and costumes.

Agricultural Beginnings

The first festivals of North America celebrated events important to an agricultural society. People planned celebrations around the harvest of a particular crop of economic and symbolic importance. When the first corn ripens in New York State each August, the Iroquois tribe demonstrates its respect for the crop in a centuries-old celebration called the Green Corn Ceremony. Preparations for the Green Corn Ceremony begin weeks in advance and involve cleaning out houses and villages, and purging possessions in an act of renewal. The ceremony begins with the lighting of a new fire on the village altar, followed by a feast of wild game and corn. Harvest festivals in towns and rural communities across North America continue to celebrate important crops. They include California's Wine Festival in Monterey; the Gilroy Garlic Festival in Gilroy, California; and the Louisiana Sugar Cane Festival in New Iberia, Louisiana.

Religious Festivals

Most festivals are of religious origin, and in North America Christian holidays and festivals dominate. Christmas, once an annual holy day set aside to commemorate the birth of Jesus Christ, is now popularized to the point that the American economy relies on the sales it generates. Other celebrations have roots in ancient European traditions. They include the Philadelphia Mummers' Day Parade, held on New Year's Day, which is based on the custom of mummers (actors) visiting people's houses to perform skits in return for food and money.

In New Orleans the French celebration of Mardi Gras (or "Fat Tuesday," the day before Ash Wednesday that begins the 40 days of Lent) is renowned for its elaborate balls, unusual costumes, floats, and street parades. Described by an 1857 New Orleans newspaper as a "vulgar and tasteless" event, Mardi Gras has continued to grow in popularity and now attracts enough revelers to deserve its reputation as America's wildest street party.

Halloween is a good example of the pre-Christian roots of many festivals. The ancient Celtic festival of *Samhain* (meaning "end of summer") was celebrated on November 1. Traditionally this was a

Day of the Dead

The Day of the Dead is a Mexican festival that celebrates both the dead and the continuity of life. It is a unique combination of Native American and Spanish influences. Originally celebrated during the Aztec month of *Miccailhuitontli* (roughly in July), Spanish priests moved the festival to coincide with All Saints' Day (November 1) in an effort to Christianize the festivities: It is now celebrated on November 1 and 2. Mexican families decorate the graves of their close ancestors and share memories of them, while enjoying a picnic that includes cookies and candies made in animal or skull shapes.

Performers in the annual New Year's Day Mummers' Parade in Philadelphia. Up to 15,000 people take part in the parade, which has been held in the city since 1901.

time when chaos ruled, when the natural order of things was disturbed, and when the unseen world had to be appeased by rituals and sacrifices. It was also a time for pranks and craziness: Men dressed as women and women as men, people's horses and livestock mysteriously moved to different fields, and children knocked on neighbors' doors for treats much in the way trick-or-treaters do today. The Christian church later created All Saints' Day (less commonly known as "All Hallows") on November 1 in an attempt to replace what they viewed as a pagan holiday. However, both festivals continued, and "Halloween" (from "All Hallows' Eve") is celebrated on the night of October 31, the day before All Saints' Day.

Ethnic Festivals

Festivals give ethnic groups a chance to celebrate their heritage. Some celebrations, such as the Irish Saint Patrick's Day, changed dramatically in style when they were brought to North America. Comunities in North America also created new festivals to celebrate the importance of an ethnic group in a particular region. Some notable examples are the Oktoberfest Zinzinnati, reflecting the large number of German immigrants in the Cincinnati, Ohio, area; the Nordic Fest in Decorah, Iowa; and the National Basque Festival in Elko, Nevada, which celebrates the traditions of the Basque people who emigrated from the Pyrenees Mountains situated between France and Spain.

New Year festivals are held at different times and are celebrated differently by various ethnic groups. Jewish Americans observe their New Year (Rosh Hashanah, Hebrew for "Beginning of the Year") in the fall with a quiet celebration. It is also known as the "Day of Atonement" because it ushers in a 10-day period of self-examination and penitence, during which Jews examine their relationship with God, the supreme judge. Because Rosh Hashanah also commemorates the creation of the world, it is also called the "Day of Remembrance." As is customary in Jewish festivals, observers begin their celebration at nightfall the day before by bathing, getting haircuts, and wearing special clothes.

In contrast, the Chinese New Year, which takes place either in January, February, or March, features parades, feasts, and decorations. Highlighted by a dragon parade, the festival is extremely loud, with gongs, cymbals, drums, and firecrackers intended to drive away the evil spirits that have accumulated throughout the year.

St. Patrick's Day

With beer flowing, "Kiss Me, I'm Irish" buttons, and leprechaun costumes, the rowdy Irish American celebration of St. Patrick, the patron saint of Ireland, eclipses its somber Irish roots. St. Patrick is credited with converting the Irish to Christianity in the fifth century A.D. He used the shamrock, a three-leafed clover, to explain the doctrine of the Holy Trinity (the union of the Father, the Son, and the Holy Ghost in one Godhead) to his converts. The first St. Patrick's Day celebration in North America took place in Boston in 1737. Today the New York St. Patrick's Day Parade is easily the largest celebration. Led by the Irish 165th Infantry and escorted by New York's prominent Irish societies, more than 150,000 marchers participate in the parade each year.

Useful websites

Smithsonian Folklife Festival (www.folklife.si.edu/CFCH/folklife)
Philadelphia Mummers' Parade (www.mummers.com/)
Day of the Dead (www.mexconnect.com/mex_/feature/daydeadindex)
Juneteenth (www.juneteenth.com/)
St. Patrick's Day (New York) (www.ny.com/holiday/stpatricks)
Searchable website for North American festivals (www.festivals.com/search/map_region.cfm?RID=n_america)

Historical Celebrations

Festivals also mark significant historical events. In the United States families celebrate Independence Day on July 4 with reunions, picnics, fireworks, and parades. Canada celebrates its National Day on July 1. Mexico's Cinco de Mayo (May 5) does not commemorate Mexican independence, but a significant battle on May 5, 1862, when a Mexican army defeated an army of French and traitor Mexicans twice its size.

A lesser-known African American festival is Juneteenth, which marks the end of slavery in Texas. On June 19, 1865, Union soldiers landed at Galveston, Texas, with news of emancipation. The news arrived two and a half years after President Lincoln's Emancipation Proclamation, and reasons for the delay remain shrouded in mystery. African Americans in Texas continued to mark the day, and many former slaves and descendants made an annual pilgrimage to Galveston. Juneteenth became increasingly popular throughout the region but remained virtually unknown outside the African American community until, in 1980, the state of Texas proclaimed Juneteenth an official holiday. A number of National Juneteenth organizations now promote appreciation of African American history and culture.

Folk Festivals

Scholars interested in cultural diversity have made a conscious effort to explore myriad different traditions in North America through establishing and running folk festivals. These festivals present grassroots arts and music to a much larger audience than their home communities. Since 1967 the Smithsonian Folklife Festival has highlighted traditions from different ethnic groups, states, and other communities for two weeks each July.

Southern belles in the annual Macy's Thanksgiving Day Parade in New York City. Staff at Macy's Department store began the parade in the 1920s, and it has become one of the city's largest celebrations.

See also

- Cultural retention (Volume 3)
- Dress and costume (Volume 3)
- Food and drink (Volume 4)
- Religion (Volume 9)

Filipinos

The Philippines are a group of Pacific islands that belonged to Spain from the 1600s until they were ceded to the United States after the Spanish–American War of 1898. Following a brief period of resistance (1899–1901) from Filipino guerrillas, the United States controlled the Philippines until 1941, when they were invaded by Japan during World War II. The United States liberated the islands in 1945 and established the independent Republic of the Philippines in 1946. The Philippines experienced further upheavals in succeeding decades, including terrorist campaigns by Marxist and Muslim guerrillas and a period of martial law (1972–1981) under the corrupt president Ferdinand Marcos, who was ousted in 1986. Today the country has returned to democratic rule but is still plagued by political instability and extremist Muslim uprisings.

Major General Edward Soriano

The first American general born in the Philippines is Major General Edward Soriano. He worked his way up through the ranks, and after graduating from the Army War College in 1989, he received his Bachelor's Degree in management from San Jose State University. He went on to earn a Master's Degree in Public Administration from the University of Missouri. Major General Soriano served in Operation Desert Shield/Storm in the Gulf War of 1991, as well as Operation Joint Endeavor in Bosnia-Herzegovina. In June 1997 he became Director of Military Support at the Department of Defense.

Filipino Americans Today

Today Filipinos are the second largest annual group of immigrants after Mexicans. In 2000 alone 42,474 Filipinos were admitted to the United States. Among the Asian American community they are second only to the Chinese in numbers. Given their rate of immigration and growth, Filipinos are expected to become the largest Asian American group within a few years. Likewise, in Canada Filipinos also comprise one of the largest immigrant communities—it is estimated at between 270,000 and 350,000 people. More than half of all Filipino Canadians live in Ontario; British Columbia, Manitoba, Alberta, and Quebec also have sizable communities. Most reside in cities: 42 percent live in Toronto and 18 percent in Vancouver.

According to the 2000 census, 69.7 percent of Filipino Americans live in the western United States. The total Filipino population nationwide as reported in the 2000 U.S. census was 1,850,314. California had nearly 50 percent of this figure, with Hawaii coming in second. An additional 12.8 percent of Filipinos live in the Northeastern, Southern, and Midwestern states. Recent immigrants to the East Coast tend to live in metropolitan areas since cities provide better employment opportunities. East Coast Filipinos are generally perceived as being part of the larger Asian American community; in contrast, West Coast Filipinos tend to live within identifiable ethnic enclaves.

Today immigrants often arrive in the United States with their families or send for them soon after arrival, so these new arrivals have been able to maintain traditional relationships, customs, and religious observances. However, Filipinos continue to suffer from social, cultural, and economic prejudice. To a certain extent civil rights legislation, court decisions, and equal

Filipino lettuce cutters at work in the fields of Imperial Valley, California, in 1939. Filipino migrant workers were an important labor force in the United States in the 1930s.

Fact File: FILIPINOS

Distribution

Most populous states
- California (almost 50%)
- Hawaii
- Florida
- Illinois
- New York
- New Jersey
- Texas
- Washington

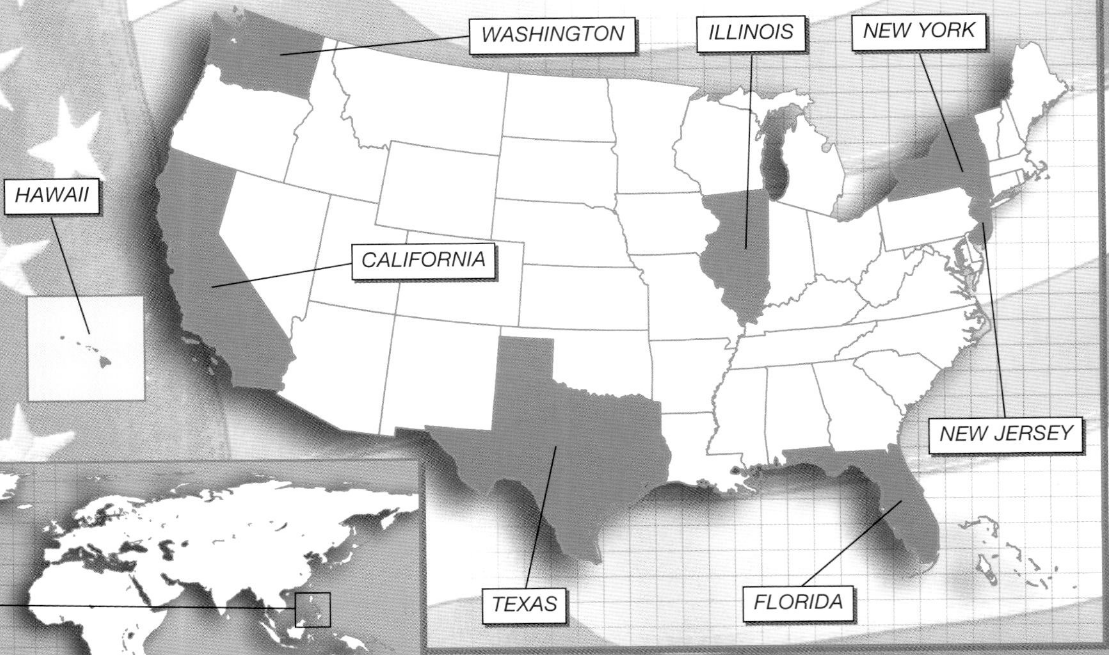

Region of origin

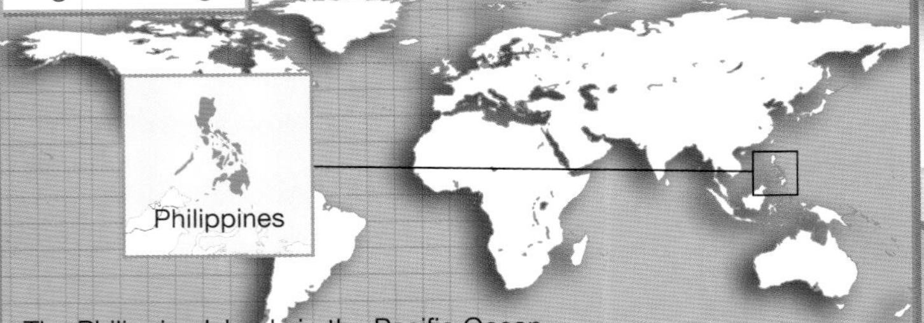

Philippines

The Philippine Islands in the Pacific Ocean.

Dates of major arrivals

- 1903–1940s (to U.S.): In 1903, through the Pensionado Act, qualified Filipino students could be sent to the United States to further their education. By 1920 there were 5,693 Filipinos living in the United States, 3,300 of them in California. In 1927, 2,869 Filipinos worked in Alaska. This number increased to 4,210 in 1930. By 1930, 45,208 Filipinos were living in the United States, and 4,000 more arrived yearly. This first wave was slowed by the start of World War II.
- 1907–1930s (to Hawaii): In 1907, 150 Filipinos arrived in Hawaii to work on the sugar plantations. By 1909, 639 workers came, and by 1910 there were 2,915. From 1911 to 1920 an estimated 3,000 workers arrived yearly. In 1919 there were 10,354 Filipinos, representing 22.9 percent of the total plantation labor force. The 1920s saw an average of 7,630 Filipinos arriving in Hawaii annually.
- Post 1945 (to Hawaii): Hawaiian plantations had a labor shortage immediately after World War II. To keep the plantations operational, the United States allowed in thousands of Filipino laborers. Around 6,000 men, 446 women, and 915 children came in 1946.
- Post 1965 (to U.S.): The Immigration and Nationality Act of 1965 allowed for a "dual chain" system of immigration consisting of "relative-selective" and "occupational" migration. Under "relative-selective immigration" Filipinos came as relatives of previous migrants who had become U.S. citizens. "Occupational" immigrants were permitted if they had skills the United States needed.

Population

U.S.: 1,850,314 (2000 census). Canada: current estimate: 270,000–350,000.

Language

Tagalog, Cubuano, and Illocano.

Community organizations

Filipino American National Historical Society (www.fanhs-national.org

National Federation of Filipino American Associations (www.naffaa.org)

Useful websites

www.filipinoweb.com/index.html provides links and information on Filipino Americans

www.filipino-americans.com gives extensive information on the Filipino community in North America, including stores, restaurants, and languages.

Festivals

Flores de Mayo (May).

Philippine Independence Day (June 12).

Rizal Day (December 30).

Food

Lumpia (an egg-roll type fingerfood filled with pork, shrimp, cabbage, beans, scallions, and bean sprouts, fried in peanut oil), *kare kare* (a peanut-oil flavored, stewed mixture of oxtail and beef tripe mixed with onions and tomatoes), and chicken and pork *adobo* (a meat sauce served over rice).

opportunity laws have worked to overturn many of the legal barriers to equality. In the early 1900s Filipinos living in California were frequently denied entry to restaurants, swimming pools, theaters, and tennis courts. Often this prejudice was based on their imperfect command of English, their darker skin tones, and media stereotyping. Today Filipinos continue to earn less than their white American counterparts and suffer greater discrimination in job markets, in spite of the fact that 43 percent of Filipino Americans have college degrees.

Filipino Immigration History

In general, Filipinos immigrated to the United States in four distinct waves. The first began in 1903 and lasted until 1940. These Filipinos, mainly young men, came to be educated. Approximately 14,000 Filipinos came to America for education between 1910 and 1938. Those who were able to gain university diplomas returned to the Philippines. Between 1907 and the 1930s the second wave of immigrants settled mainly in Hawaii to work in the fields. The third wave in the 1940s and 1950s was inspired by difficulties in the new Philippine Republic and the desire for a better life in the United States. By 1960 Hawaii had 69,070 Filipinos, and California had 65,459. Together they contained 76 percent of the Filipino American population. The fourth wave, and by far the largest and most skilled, occurred after 1970 and continues today. According to the 2000 census, the United States has 1,850,314 people of Filipino descent. The Philippines has become the leading foreign provider of accountants, engineers, nurses, physicians, teachers, and technical workers in the United States. Women in particular are employed as healthcare and domestic workers in the United States and in Canada.

Filipino Communities—Then and Now

Filipino immigrants to the United States have always been a minority set apart. Before 1946 they could not acquire American citizenship unless they had served in the United States military for three years and received an honorable discharge. The inability to gain citizenship made it impossible for Filipinos to gain state licenses to practice in law, medicine, and other professions.

The Filipino community did not begin to grow until immigrants began to settle and marry Americans. Many of those in the first and second waves of immigration returned home. However, those who stayed began a vibrant community that gradually became centered on the Roman Catholic church. In the beginning the young men arriving between 1913 and the 1930s were often unable to marry Filipino women, since they outnumbered them 14 to 1. California had passed a law in 1905 denying peoples it termed "Mongolians" (which included all Asian immigrants) the right to marry white women. By 1936 the states of Nevada, Oregon, and Washington had passed

Filipinos in showbusiness

Many Filipino Americans or Americans of Filipino descent are active in Hollywood: Tia Carrere (below) appeared in the movie *Wayne's World*; Lou Diamond Phillips rose to stardom in *La Bamba*, *Courage under Fire*, and *Brokedown Palace*; and Rob Schneider gained fame for his work in comedies such as *Home Alone 2: Lost in New York*, *Deuce Bigalow: Male Gigolo*, *Big Daddy*, and *The Animal*. Other famous Filipino Americans in entertainment include Nia Peoples and Tamlyn Tomita, .

Women in traditional costume dance on the streets of New York City during the Philippine Day Parade held every June to mark Filipino independence.

similar laws. Instead, many Filipinos married Mexican or Puerto Rican women. Filipinos continued to live with white women, but the women had only the status of common law wives until 1946, when the Supreme Court found that the state laws violated individual civil rights. Since Filipino men married outside their ethnic group, many Americans felt antagonism toward them. White resentment of the attention Filipinos paid white women, coupled with fears that Filipinos were taking white jobs, led to stereotyping and prejudice.

Filipinos traditionally depended on family groups for sustenance and financial assistance. Since this type of community could not be continued in North America due to the lack of women, men joined *barrios*, or communities, to cook, eat, and live. These surrogate families were headed by the eldest man of the household.

The second wave of Filipino immigrants soon realized that a combination of difficulties with English, white prejudice, and limited job skills kept them from well-paid employment. However, even low-paying jobs paid better in the United States than in the Philippines, and so Filipinos became migratory field hands and cannery workers. Usually these jobs were seasonal, but permanent jobs were available to some Filipinos who opened shops or who worked in hotels and restaurants. However, the higher wages were often offset by the higher cost of living, stranding many Filipinos in America who would have otherwise returned to the Philippines.

Filipino Arts and Culture

Filipino culture remains vibrant within immigrant communities. Most host annual dances and cooking demonstrations for the general public. Gambling and gaming are also popular. Wearing the Philippine national costume at dances, on national holidays and at weddings is a tradition. While weddings were often small affairs during the early waves of immigration, today elaborate wedding celebrations rival those held in the Philippines.

The most distinctive cultural aspect within the Filipino American community is the use of language. Most Filipinos speak Illocano, Cubuano, or Tagalog. Each of these languages derives from a separate province of the Philippines. The speakers of each language form separate community groups, since regional identification is more important than national association to Filipino people. Filipino writers, such as Carlos Bulosan and Jose Rizal, a Philippine national hero, remain popular.

See also

- Immigrant experience (Volume 5)
- Intermarriage (Volume 5)
- Language retention (Volume 6)
- Pacific Islanders (Volume 8)

Film

The film industry in the United States is probably the most vibrant and innovative in the world. From its very beginnings the images produced in Hollywood, California, did much to provide the world with its ideas and beliefs about the United States as a nation, and the movies became a focus of attention for the millions of immigrants who flocked to American shores, each hoping to fulfill the dreams of wealth and freedom that they saw portrayed on the silver screen.

The Movie Industry Is Born

In 1884 a New York peepshow became the first commercial movie "theater." A few seconds of moving images inside a box, called a "kinetoscope," viewed by one person at a time, proved novel enough that "kinetoscope parlors" opened in many American cities.

In 1908 the Motion Picture Patents Company (MPPC) was formed to control all aspects of film production and distribution. At the same time, a number of independent producers and distributors moved from the East Coast to the Hollywood area of Los Angeles, California, for its ideal climate for daylight filming, cheap property, and open space on which to build movie sets. By 1912, 15 film companies were operating in Hollywood. Many were headed by urban first- or second-generation immigrants, such as Russian-born Louis B. Mayer and Sam Goldwyn, a Polish immigrant. These men recognized the movie industry as a fast way to earn money, respectability, and power.

Origins of the stars

Some of Hollywood's biggest stars were or are immigrants, having been born outside the United States. This list shows their country of origin:

Antonio Banderas, Spain.
Ingrid Bergman, Sweden.
Yul Brynner, Soviet Union.
John Candy, Canada.
Charlie Chaplin, England.
Sean Connery, Scotland.
Russell Crowe, New Zealand.
Marlene Dietrich, Germany.
Michael J. Fox, Canada.
Audrey Hepburn, Belgium.
Anthony Hopkins, Wales.
Peter Lorre, Hungary.
Liam Neeson, Ireland.
Anthony Quinn, Mexico.
Arnold Schwarzenegger, Austria.
Omar Sharif, Egypt.
Rudolph Valentino, Italy.
Catherine Zeta-Jones, Wales.

The Golden Age of Silent Movies

The golden era of silent movies ran from approximately 1910 to 1925. One figure more than any other in this period personified the American experience for the millions of new immigrants to North America—Charlie Chaplin's "Little Tramp." From 1914 to 1924 Chaplin, an English immigrant, appeared in many films in many guises but always with the same traits of innocence and optimism that struck a chord with new arrivals to the United States. Silent movies meant there were no language barriers to confuse Chaplin's view of the common man seeking his destiny in a new land. Simple and sentimental, these films captivated the first generation of American moviegoers as no others did.

The immigrant businessmen of Hollywood's early years seemed to know what the masses wanted, but they created entertainment that

Leo the lion being recorded in 1928 for the trademark of Metro-Goldwyn-Mayer movie company. The studio was run by two immigrants—Sam Goldwyn and Louis B. Mayer.

Marlon Brando as a Mafia boss in The Godfather *(1972). The film depicted life in an Italian American crime family.*

mirrored stereotypes of the day. Every ethnic group had its stock characters, and no color or race was exempt. In what may now seem a bizarre practice, most of the important ethnic characters pre-1940 were played by made-up white actors. Technicians' manuals of the period detailed how to create "blackface," "yellowface," or "warpaint." Some moviemakers even claimed that whites made better minorities because they played the roles as stereotypes, while minority actors tried to play the roles realistically.

Reflecting Society's Changes

Film became America's most popular and influential form of cultural media, reflecting the social climate of the time. The advent of sound and, later, color meant that film could have an even greater impact on its audience. A production code, in place from the mid-1930s to the 1960s, ensured that acceptable ideologies were promoted through mainstream film. This was taken to extremes, however, in the late 1940s and 1950s when, at the height of the Cold War and McCarthyism, the House Un-American Activities Committee made a blacklist of left-wing and communist sympathizers who were then forbidden to work in Hollywood. Many were jailed, and many fled the country in exile.

After World War II the portrayal of minorities slowly began to change. Movies began to show African Americans as war heroes, and in the liberal 1960s interracial relationships became movie subjects, as seen in *Guess Who's Coming to Dinner* with Sidney Poitier (1967). At the same time, a new generation of African American filmmakers reflected growing black militancy through "blaxploitation" films such as *Shaft*, starring black actor Richard Roundtree. *The Godfather* (1972), starring Marlon Brando, delved into lives of second-generation Italian Americans at a time when the Italian American Mafia was making headlines.

Recent Developments

In the 1980s many film studios were taken over by multinational conglomerates, which may have helped broaden Hollywood's ethnic horizons. In recent years new technology has made independent filmmaking easier, and minority groups are finding new voices and reaching larger audiences. Creative talents like African American director Spike Lee have brought a fresh approach to filmmaking, and independent film festivals throughout America provide wider exposure for the work of minority groups. Mexican, Native, and Asian American filmmakers are just a few of the groups producing some of today's most innovative films. In 2002 Halle Berry became the first black actress to win the Academy Award for Best Actress for her role in *Monster's Ball*, a film in which race issues are a central theme. From its origins more than a century ago, American film continues to develop and to increasingly reflect the nation's multicultural society.

Jewish moviemakers

The first "talking picture" was *The Jazz Singer* in 1927, starring Al Jolson, a Jewish immigrant, in a story of a cantor's son who becomes a stage star. The movie was not only a triumph of technical innovation; the subject matter also underlined the prominence of Jewish influence in Hollywood that has continued ever since. Other Jewish filmmakers include David O. Selznick, who was responsible for the epic *Gone with the Wind* (1939); Stanley Kubrick, whose *2001: A Space Odyssey* (1968) remains a classic science-fiction film; and Steven Spielberg, who directed another classic fantasy *E.T.: The Extra-Terrestrial* (1982).

See also

- Broadcasting (Volume 2)
- Jews (Volume 6)
- Literature (Volume 6)

Finns

The country of Finland is one of the Baltic nations of northern Europe. For centuries Finland was a province of neighboring Sweden, but in 1809 it became part of the Russian Empire. In 1917 Finland became independent. Its population comprises a Finnish-speaking majority and a Swedish-speaking minority (6 percent). Migrants to North America are usually Finnish-speakers. Today there are more than 600,000 Finnish Americans in the United States and about 100,000 Finnish Canadians in Canada.

A scarcity of good farm land, population growth, and political pressure from the Russian Empire resulted in an increase in emigration from Finland in the late 19th and early 20th centuries. A second wave of emigration took place after World War II, principally to Canada.

Farmers gathering in hay in western Massachusetts at the turn of the 19th and 20th centuries. Massachusetts attracted early Finnish immigrants, many of whom were farmers.

Most Finnish Americans came from a rural background, with only a small number having industrial experience. They settled mainly in the northern parts of the United States. In Washington, Oregon, and California they were employed as farmers, lumberjacks, fishermen, and even miners in the Rocky Mountains. They were also attracted to the farmland in Michigan and Minnesota, and in Massachusetts, New York, Ohio, and Pennsylvania to the factories as well. Canadian Finns settled on the shores of the Great Lakes. The largest centers in Canada have traditionally been in the Sudbury copper mining district, the Thunder Bay (earlier Port Arthur) area with its lumbering and farming, the British Columbia and Vancouver areas, and the cities of Montreal, Toronto, and Quebec.

More than 60 percent of Finns who settled in North America were young males, while 40 percent were females. Finnish immigrant women were generally employed as domestic servants.

Waves of Migration

Between 1638 and 1656 settlers in the New Sweden colony in Delaware included several hundred Finns. However, the major waves of Finnish immigration occurred between 1870 and 1930, when 321,700 Finns emigrated to the United States. Between 1901 and 1930 a further 68,200 Finns emigrated to Canada. In 1930 economic recession in both countries curtailed immigration. After World War II Canada admitted a large number of Finns who had lost their homes and livelihoods when large parts of Finland were taken over by the Soviet Union. Canada has continued to be more accessible to Finns than the United States, which has adhered to strict immigration quotas. The number of Finns who emigrated to Canada between 1951 and 1970 was 22,500. Today the United States receives a few hundred Finns per year, many of whom have qualifications from higher education.

Useful websites

The Finnish American and Finnish Canadian Organization provides names of Suomi (Finland) societies (www.finn.st/orgs).

The Immigration History Research Center of the University of Minnesota provides information on Finnish Americans and their descendants (www.umn.edu/ihrc).

Finnish–American Chamber of Commerce (www.finlandtrade.com)

Finlandia Foundation (www.finlandiafoundation.org)

Fact File: FINNS

Distribution

- Michigan: 109,300, or 16.5%
- Minnesota: 103,600, or 15.7%
- California: 64,300, or 10%
- Washington: 44,000, or 6.6%
- Massachusetts 31,500, or 4.7%
- Florida: 25,000, or 3.7%
- Oregon: 22,900, or 3.4%
- New York: 21,300, or 3.2%
- Ohio: 21,100, or 3.1%

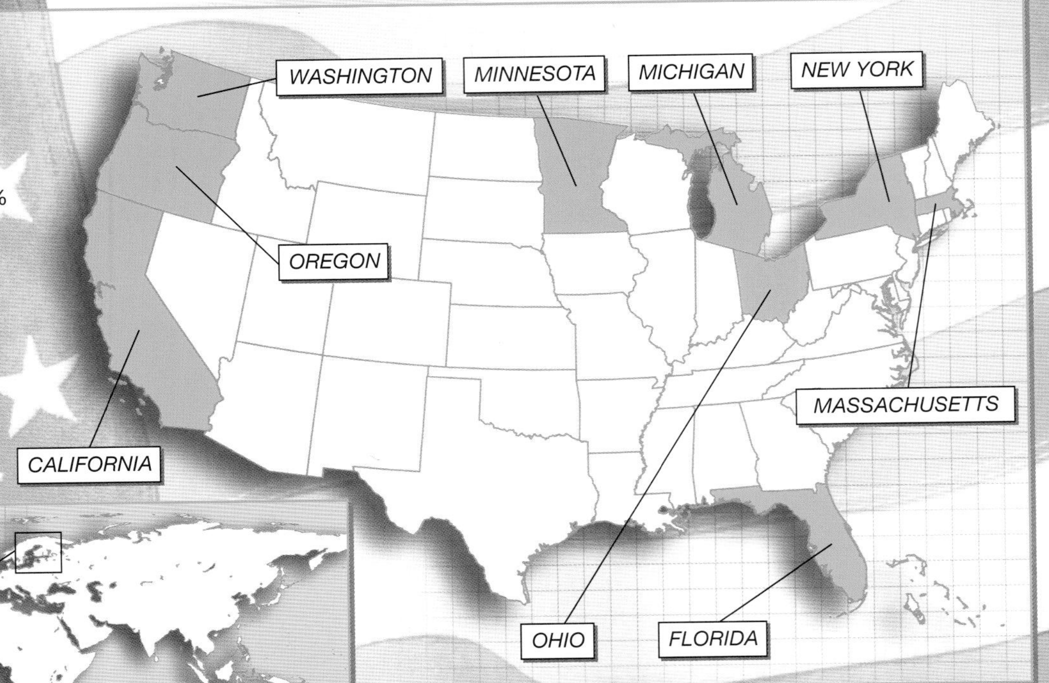

Region of origin

Finland

Finland is a country in northern Europe on the shores of the Baltic Sea.

Dates of major arrivals

- United States

1638–1656: Several hundred Finns came to the New Sweden Colony in Delaware.

1870–1930: 321,700 Finns emigrated to the United States. The highest number came in 1902, when 23,000 Finnish immigrants arrived.

- Canada

1901–1920: 32,200 Finns emigrated to Canada.

1921–1930: 36,000 Finns emigrated to Canada.

1951–1970: 22,500 Finns emigrated to Canada.

Community organizations

Association and community activities used to be plentiful and included temperance groups, churches, cultural associations (ideological and nonideological), historical societies, workers' "hall societies" (groups), and cooperatives. Some still flourish, including the Finlandia Foundation and Suomi (Finland) Societies.

Names

Many Finnish names are connected with nature such as Mäki (meaning "hill"); names ending in *–nen* point to a place. For example, Koskinen means someone from the *koski* (the falls).

Population

In the United States, at least 579,000 people have one grandparent of Finnish origin (2000 estimate). In Canada there are 91,300 people of Finnish descent according to 1986 figures.

Language

English is now the first language of almost all Finnish Americans. As late as the early 20th century Finnish immigrants spoke Finnish, which belongs to the Finno-Ugric linguistic group.

Jobs

The first Finnish immigrants were farmers, lumber workers, miners, and domestic servants. Later Finnish Americans moved to skilled and urban professions. The second, third, and fourth generations often desired higher education and became teachers and professionals with a college education.

Religion

Protestant Christianity, including Evangelical Lutheran, Apostolic Lutheran, and various free churches.

Festivals

All major Christian festivals.
Independence Day of Finland (December 6).
St. Urho's Day (March 16).
Midsummer (June 24).

Food

Mojakka (stew), soups, meat, porridge, fish, natural berries, root vegetables, rye breads, *pulla* (wheat cake).

Cultural Life

A fairly high percentage of Finnish Americans maintain their heritage, with celebrations such as Midsummer Day (June 24) and Finnish Independence Day (December 6). Other festivals have gained in popularity, such as Laskiainen (Shrovetide), the festival of St. Urho (March 16), and events like the Grand Finn Fest held in 2000 in Toronto.

Educational facilities working to preserve the Finnish language in the United States include the Salolampi (Minnesota) Finnish language summer camp and the Finlandia University (formerly known as the Suomi College) in Hancock, Michigan. There are several Finnish-language publications that are remnants of the once powerful Finnish-American and Finnish-Canadian press, such as *Finnish-American Reporter* and *Raivaaja* in the United States and *Vapaa Sana* in Canada.

In the early 1900s many Finnish Americans held politically radical views, but few traces remain today. Early Finnish immigrants established hundreds of cooperative shops, especially in the Great Lakes region, plus a large central organization. Some of these ventures remain and continue the tradition of community effort that was invaluable to new immigrants trying to make a living. In North America there are a number of Suomi (Finland) Societies and branches of the Finnish-American Chamber of Commerce. One of the most influential organizations is the Finlandia Foundation, which has branches in at least 14 states.

Finnish men outside a traditional sauna or steam house. Early Finnish immigrants introduced saunas to North America, building them on to their new farm houses.

Notable Finnish Americans

Emil Hurja, Democrat strategist and politician of the 1930s.
Jessica Lange, actress
Oscar J. Larson, Member of the House of Representatives.
John Morton, signatory of the Declaration of Independence of the United States.
Ville Ritola, multiple Olympic Games gold medalist in athletics.
Eero Saarinen, architect.
Linus Torwalds, computer developer.

Finnish American Communities

In the course of a few generations Finns have become primarily urban and are concentrated in a number of major urban areas in the United States and Canada. The states of Florida and California have become centers for retired Finnish Americans and have also attracted recent Finnish immigration. The high rate of assimilation among Finns means that, in most parts of the United States, membership in Finnish organizations is declining. Most of the original Finnish-speaking societies, churches, and cultural associations are now English-speaking, but Finnish religious associations are still very active, even when they have adopted the English language. In Canada, especially in Toronto, Sudbury, Thunder Bay, Vancouver, and surrounding areas, Finnish community life is more vibrant than in the United States because of the continuing trickle of new immigrants.

See also

- Agriculture (Volume 1)
- Danes (Volume 3)
- Norwegians (Volume 8)
- Swedes (Volume 10

Folklore

Useful websites

Latin-American Folklore Resources (http://latino.sscnet.ucla.edu/research/folklore.html)
American Folklore Society (http://afsnet.org)
American Folklore (www.americanfolklore.net)
Native American Indian Folklore (www.earthbow.com/native)
Folklore and Mythology (www.djmcadam.com/folklore.html)
Regional Folklore and Mythology (www.pibburns.com/mythregi.htm)
American Folklife Center at the Library of Congress (http://lcweb.loc.gov/folklife)

Folklore is the informal cultural knowledge that is transmitted from person to person within families or communities rather than through formal education, books, or the media. The diverse ethnic communities of North America are rich in these traditions and have inherited from their immigrant ancestors a vast depth of folklore from around the world. In addition, folklore plays an integral part in the lives of Native American peoples.

There are many types of folklore, which can be divided into genres: architecture; arts and crafts, including folk costume; music and dance; verbal arts like jokes, stories, and poetry; drama; festivals and celebrations; beliefs and superstitions; and foodways (how and what people eat and cook). Some folklore is associated with a specific ethnic group, like Mexican *mariachi* music or the Irish St. Patrick's Day celebrations, and some may be associated with a particular profession, like fishermen who make artwork with seashells or lumberjacks who carve wooden sculptures using chainsaws.

Scholar William Bascom wrote that folklore serves four main functions. First, it may be used as entertainment, like popular dance music. Second, it can validate culture by explaining why it is the way it is, as do many myths. Third, morals and values can be taught to children through proverbs (for example, "Waste not, want not") and fables. Finally, folklore can help maintain social conformity by expressing disapproval of those who break the rules (as seen in the folk story "The Boy Who Cried Wolf") or by expressing approval for those who uphold cultural values.

Native American Folklore

The United States and Canada are home to more than 1,100 officially recognized Native American groups, each with its own very different languages and customs. A few items of folklore are common cross-culturally, and some have been adopted relatively recently as symbols of a new pan-Indian ethnic consciousness. For example, the foodstuff frybread—a kind of large popover topped with meat, beans, and honey—is common to many native peoples. Similarly powwows—large gatherings of many tribes featuring traditional dance and music—are held annually. Other common traditions include "trickster" tales in which a character violates cultural taboos to humorous effect while providing a moral lesson for the listening audience.

The Arapaho Ghost Dance of the late 19th century. The Ghost Dance was a powerful influence among Native Americans at the time, since it was believed that it would bring about the restoration of tribal rights and the end of white rule.

Another important part of Native American culture is the "creation myth." Almost all Native American peoples have their own beliefs on how the world was created. These stories often have elements in common, such as emergence from an underground world. This is the myth of the Mandan Sioux and the Mojave Apache:

"The earliest people lived under the ground near a beautiful lake. Once, a great grapevine grew above their home. A root from the grapevine poked down into the village of the underground people. A few of the most courageous then climbed the vine into the world above. When these explorers returned, they reported that the world above was more beautiful than anything they had imagined, teeming with fish and game, full of light and beautiful flowers. Soon large numbers of people began climbing the vine into the new world above.

One day, however, an obese woman began to climb, and the root broke, leaving half of the people underground, where they remain to this day. When we die, we rejoin our cousins under the earth." (www.geocities.com/RainForest/Canopy/7979/indian/)

In addition to myths, arts and crafts like Pueblo pottery, Navajo rugmaking, and the basketmaking of various tribes are all part of the folklore of individual native peoples and, in many cases, have become significant modern sources of income for those groups.

Immigrant Folklore

Each successive wave of immigrants to North America has brought its own folklore to the New World. Many early immigrants to the United States and Canada came from the British Isles. Englishwomen, in particular, practiced needlecrafts like knitting, lacemaking, and quilting that are still carried on today. Irish musical traditions contributed to the development of Appalachian music like "old-time" and bluegrass, and today's Irish American communities are reviving interest in traditional step dancing. Some descendants of Scottish immigrants have similarly renewed an interest in Highland dancing and in the playing of traditional Scottish music on bagpipes.

African Americans have had perhaps the biggest influence of any minority group on North American popular culture. African American wordplay and slang infuse the everyday speech of Americans and Canadians of all ethnicities. Traditional types of music like blues and spirituals led to the development of jazz, rock, and gospel, which in turn gave rise to new styles like hip-hop—all of which are now heard around the world.

Halloween

Also known as All Hallows Eve, Halloween on October 31 is one of the richest and most obvious forms of folklore that has found its way into mainstream American life. Immigrants to America, particularly the Irish and Scottish, introduced many Halloween traditions such as "trick or treating" and the carving of pumpkin lanterns. Halloween is a time for witches, ghosts, goblins, and demons, since it was originally thought of as being the one time in the year when evil spirits could walk the earth.

For more information on the folklore and origins of Halloween visit the Happy Halloween website at www.rumela.com/events/events_october_halloween.htm

An early movie version of the Golem story, which is a part of Eastern European Jewish folklore. The Golem was a mythical clay man summoned into life in much the same way as Frankenstein's monster, and with similarly chaotic results.

See also

- African Americans (Volume 1)
- Crafts (Volume 3)
- Cultural retention (Volume 3)
- Festivals (Volume 4)
- Food and drink (Volume 4)
- Jews (Volume 6)
- Sioux (Volume 9)

Jewish Traditions

Jewish people came to North America from many parts of the world—chiefly Europe, the Middle East, and North Africa—and have different folklore traditions that reflect their national origins. Eastern European Jews, for example, tell the story of the Golem. In medieval Jewish legend the Golem was an automatonlike servant made of clay and given life by means of a charm, or "shem." Golem myths were attributed to several rabbis in a number of eastern European countries. The most famous version was centered around Rabbi Löw in 16th-century Prague. After molding the Golem and endowing it with life, Rabbi Löw was forced to destroy the clay creature after it ran amok—the moral of the story being that only God can bestow the gift of life with impunity.

Other Jewish folklore centers on the practices of the Jewish religion, Judaism. Jews celebrate the same religious holidays, like Passover and Rosh Hashanah, but often do so in different ways. For example, many Jews of European origin make the traditional Passover food *charoset* from apples and walnuts, while those from the Middle East often use figs and dates.

Hispanic Folklore

Hispanic Americans trace their roots to Spanish-speaking countries, each with a unique body of folklore. One such tradition is the Mexican holiday of *Cinco de Mayo*. This festival commemorates May 5, 1862, the day when forces of the Mexican President Benito Juárez defeated an invading French army. It is a good occasion to show pride in being Mexican and is celebrated throughout Mexico and by those of Mexican descent. Parades and reenactments of the battle are held, and there is dancing to music from Mexican *mariachi* bands. In most Mexican towns fairs are held at which people enjoy the rides and play games. *Cinco de Mayo* ends with traditional shouts of "¡Viva México!"

Another part of Mexican folklore is the birthday tradition of breaking piñatas. The piñata, a container usually made from papier mâché in the form of an animal, is filled with candy and hung from the ceiling. The birthday child is blindfolded and hits out with a stick to crack the piñata open. All the children present then share the gifts inside. Also, when a Mexican girl reaches the age of 15, her birthday is celebrated with a special Catholic mass. A party is given to introduce her as a young woman, and she dances a waltz with her father. Many Mexican American communities continue these customs, especially in the American Southwest.

A child being blindfolded before breaking open a piñata at his birthday party in a Mexican American community in Nebraska. He will hit out with his stick to break open the piñata, causing the candy inside to cascade out.

Food and drink

Food and drink are essential for life; they are also a central part of human culture. Growing, farming, and harvesting food, preparing and cooking ingredients, and eating habits and rituals have both shaped the way different groups of people live and also reflected their values and beliefs. The food and drink of different peoples are influenced by environment and climate as well as by factors such as religious beliefs and wealth. From the 20th century they have also been influenced by improvements in long-distance transportation, refrigeration, mass-production, and distribution. Modern supermarkets make processed foods, ready meals, and foods from around the world available all year round.

Traditional American Food

North America is home to a remarkably wide array of different food and drink, reflecting both its varied environment and its diverse immigrant population. The question of what is typical American food is not an easy one to answer. While traditionally it might have been a meal of meat and potatoes or the Thanksgiving turkey dinner and sweet pumpkin pie, today the type of food most associated with America is "fast food"—fries, hamburgers, and soft drinks. Yet the situation is much more complex, particularly in urban centers, which have always attracted immigrants. In most cities food from every country in the world—from Lebanese to Indian to Japanese to Thai to Hungarian to African—is easily obtainable.

Because mealtimes are often private family times, food is usually one of the last aspects of immigrant culture to be assimilated into a broader U.S. lifestyle. It is often viewed as an important part of a group's identity and usually features in festivals. Stores carrying specific ethnic foods are often social gathering places in new immigrant communities and, with ethnic cafés and restaurants, also help bring new foods to a wider audience.

Regional and Ethnic Foods

The vast range of physical geography and climate in North America, and the resulting bounty of food, have contributed to make it a true "land of plenty." Indian corn (maize), wild rice, turkey, buffalo, deer, elk, moose, cod, salmon, sturgeon, lobster, crab, clams, blueberries, cranberries, tomatoes, beans, chili peppers, pumpkins, squash, and maple syrup are just a few foods indigenous to North America. Others were introduced by early European settlers—wheat, cattle, hogs, sheep, apples, apricots, carrots, lentils, peaches, purslane, and turnips, as well as potatoes and sugar from South America. The

Fast food

The history of fast food in America began in 1921, when Walter Andersen founded the first Whitecastle hamburger restaurant in Wichita, Kansas. He sold a hamburger sandwich with fries and a cola for 5 cents. By 1930 there were 116 restaurants in the chain. The next development came in 1948, when Richard and Maurice MacDonald opened a new type of fast-food restaurant with no indoor tables or waitresses, where customers were encouraged to order their food through a window and to eat in their cars. The success of MacDonalds soon inspired many other burger chains, including Burger King and Wendy's.

Many different types of food are available on this street in New York City, including Italian, Chinese, and meat butchered according to the kosher laws of the Jewish faith.

The traditional Thanksgiving dinner commemorates the feast held by the Pilgrim Fathers to celebrate their first successful fall harvest in Plymouth, Massachusetts.

process is ongoing, as new immigrants from around the world continually introduce foods from their homelands. Some regions of America are still closely identified with foods that flourish there: salmon is associated with Washington state, lobster with Maine, clams with New England, wine with California, and maple syrup with Vermont.

Blending Culinary Traditions

Successive groups of immigrants have also introduced new ways of preparing and cooking food, often combining their own traditions with those they find in the United States. Today the blending of different culinary traditions is often called "fusion food." While the food of early European immigrants was influenced by the dishes they had eaten at home in England, Germany, Holland, France, and Spain, the food of their African slaves was influenced not only by their varied traditions but also by the very limited ingredients they were allowed. The type of African American cooking now known as "soul food" grew out of slave dishes based on green leafy vegetables and poor cuts of meat, and includes gumbos, meat stews thickened with okra (introduced from Africa) and eaten with rice; "greens," vegetables such as chard, collard greens, kale, and spinach cooked for a long time and flavored with meat; and fried meat and chicken. Another long-established "fusion food" is Tex-Mex, which probably dates from the mid-19th century and combines Mexican and Spanish influences to create spicy flavors. Chili con carne, a bean-and-beef stew flavored with hot chili powder, is the best known Tex-Mex dish. One of the most recent "fusion foods" to emerge is the Pacific Rim style, which combines California health trends toward fresh ingredients with Southeast Asian flavors and cooking techniques such as stir-frying.

Popular Tradition

Despite the wealth of new ingredients and cooking styles brought to North America by different immigrant groups, the most ubiquitous foods of the 20th and 21st centuries are undoubtedly fast food, ice creams, and soft drinks such as colas. Practically all immigrant groups modify their diet to include sweet drinks and ice creams, and the popularity of a cheap meal of burgers and fries served instantaneously and wrapped to take out has swept the world since its invention in 1920s America.

Useful websites

EatEthnic, for information on ethnic ingredients, recipes, and traditions (http://eatethnic.com)

World in Your Kitchen, site with excellent links for international and American cooking (www.creative-homeliving.com/World-Kitchen/home.htm)

SOAR, site with over 45,000 recipes from around the world (http://soar.berkeley.edu/recipes)

See also

- Agriculture (Volume 1)
- Cultural retention (Volume 3)
- Festivals (Volume 4)
- Health and healing (Volume 5)

French

French Americans do not fit the usual pattern of immigration in North America. Some French immigrants arrived in groups, but many came as individuals in search of opportunity. Ambitious and highly skilled, the French have been successful in North America. Although their recent immigration numbers have been relatively low, the French have greatly influenced North American society.

Early French Americans

The French had a very early presence in North America. The French explorer Jacques Cartier first laid claim to territories along the St. Lawrence River in Canada in 1534. Samuel de Champlain followed nearly 70 years later and established the colony of Quebec in 1608. As early as the 1550s the Huguenot sailor Jean Ribaut attempted to establish French Huguenot (Protestant) colonies near Beaufort, South Carolina, and Jacksonville, Florida.

The French also explored the waterways of North America. By 1620—the year the English Pilgrims landed at Plymouth—French explorers had discovered three of the Great Lakes and later established the outposts of Detroit and St. Louis. In 1673 Jacques Marquette and Louis Jolliet traveled southward on the Mississippi River until they reached the Arkansan Indian tribes. Robert Cavelier de La Salle followed in 1682, traveling the length of the Mississippi to the Gulf of Mexico, where he claimed the entire Mississippi Valley for the King of France. In 1718 Jean-Baptiste Bienville founded the French colony of New Orleans. At its peak at the turn of the 17th and 18th centuries New France included eastern Canada, the Great Lakes, and the valleys of the Ohio and Mississippi rivers.

E.I. Dupont

Éleuthère Irénée du Pont (1771–1834) was born in Paris and worked in his father's printing plant until it was destroyed in the French Revolution. He emigrated to America in 1800 and established a gunpowder factory in Wilmington, Delaware. The factory grew quickly during the 1812 war, establishing the success of E.I. DuPont de Nemours & Co. Under the management of his heirs DuPont Chemical–General Motors has become one of the largest industrial corporations in history.

A 16th-century painting of Native Americans worshiping a column erected by the French explorer Jean Ribaut in Florida in 1562.

Fact File: FRENCH

Distribution

Most populous states:

- California
- Massachusetts
- New York
- Texas
- Louisiana
- Ohio

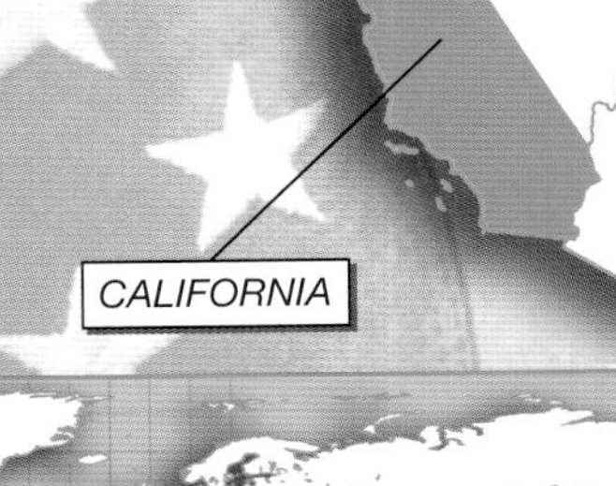

Region of origin

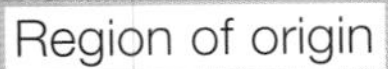

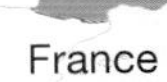

Many French immigrants to North America have come directly from France, though some have also come via other regions like the Caribbean.

Population

- United States: The total population of French Americans excluding Basques is 9,775,761 (2000 U.S. census).
- Canada: The total population of Canadians with French as their mother tongue is 6,636,660.

Notable French Americans

John James Audubon, naturalist.
Pierre Boulez, composer.
Octave Chanute, engineer.
Claudette Colbert, actress.
Jacques Cousteau, marine explorer.
E.I. Dupont, industrialist.
Thomas Gallaudet, educator.
John Jay, first Chief Justice of the U.S. Supreme Court.
Pierre Charles L'Enfant, architect and engineer.
Henry Wadsworth Longfellow, poet.
Paul Revere, silversmith famous for his role in the American Revolution.
Edna St. Vincent Millay, poet.

First immigrants

- 1534: Jacques Cartier traveled the St. Lawrence River
- 1550s: Huguenot settlements in South Carolina and Florida.
- 1608: Quebec settled by Samuel de Champlain.

Dates of major arrivals

- 1686–1760: Huguenots fleeing persecution in France.
- 1849–1851: Attracted by the California Gold Rush.

Jobs

A high proportion of French Americans hold managerial and professional positions, as well being employed in technical, sales, and administrative occupations.

Religion

Mainly Roman Catholicism. Some Protestants, who are descendants of French Huguenots who later joined the Anglican church (the Church of England).

Names

Arnauld (Arnold), Bernard, Bertrand, Chevalier, David, de Forest, DeLancey, Gaylord, Jay, Rivoire (Revere).

Festivals

All major Christian festivals.
Bastille Day (July 14).
Mardi Gras ("Fat Tuesday," the day before the beginning of Lent, usually in February).

Community organizations

French American Foundation (www.frenchamerican.org)
French Institute/Alliance Française (www.fiaf.org)
National Huguenot Society (www.huguenot.netnation.com/general)

Food

Omelet, quiche, soufflé, fondue, French bread (baguettes), mousse, pâté, champagne, wine.

Many of the first French to come to North America were fur traders called *coureurs des bois* ("runners of the woods"), who traded with the Native Americans during the westward expansion of New France. In Canada the Métis are descendants of these early French immigrants and Native American women. Métis communities today, particularly in Canada, have a strong sense of ethnic identity. Other early Frenchmen were Jesuit missionaries who came to convert the Native Americans to Catholicism.

Although there were many French outposts in North America by the late 17th century, French communities were sparse; only the settlements of Quebec, Illinois, and Louisiana were of any consequence. Illinois grew into a strong farming region, while Louisiana had to contend with the local native peoples in the Natchez Wars. New Orleans grew slowly, with the French bringing black slaves from Haiti to augment the workforce in the region.

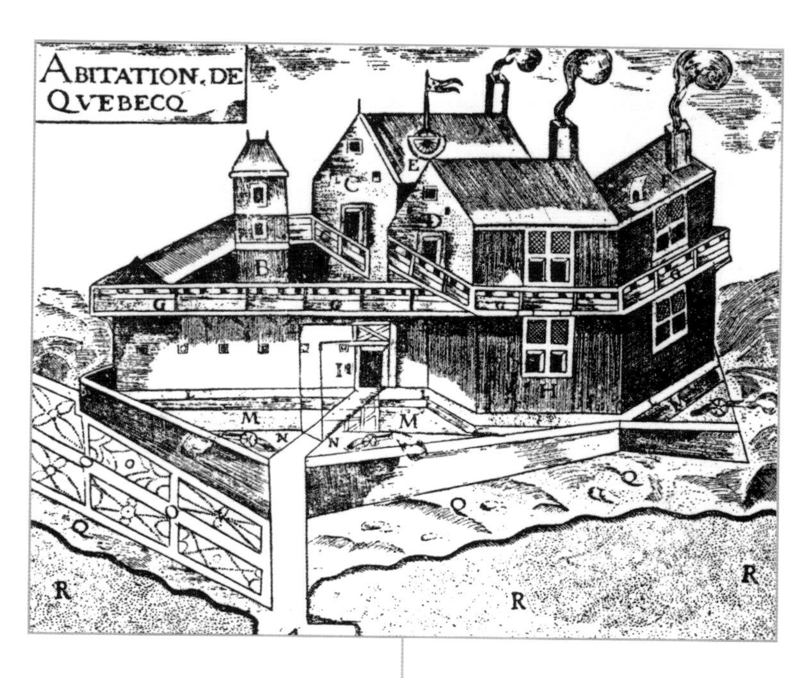

A drawing made in 1629 showing the early French colony of Quebec, Canada. The French explorer Samuel de Champlain favored Quebec as a site for the capital of New France because of its location on the St. Lawrence River.

Huguenots

The earliest group of French immigrants to North America were French Protestants known as Huguenots, who faced religious persecution in their homeland. As early as the mid-1500s the Huguenots felt threatened by French Catholics and left France for other countries, including North America. When Louis XVI revoked the Edict of Nantes in 1685, banning Protestantism in France, the flow of Huguenots to North America and other European countries became a flood.

By the 1760s some 14,000 Huguenots had come to the 13 British colonies. Their most significant settlements were in South Carolina (where they made up 4 percent of the colony's population), in and around New York City (particularly in New Rochelle, Harlem, and Staten Island), in Massachusetts, and in Virginia. The majority of the Huguenots in North America were skilled workers, and many rose to prominence as craftsmen, merchants, and businessmen.

The Huguenots tended to assimilate well into the culture of the American colonies, accepting North America as their new homeland. Many Huguenots changed their names to sound more English: Rivoire became Revere, Baudouin became Bowdoin, and Boileau became Drinkwater. Huguenot congregations, which were once independent, fairly quickly became French-language parishes of the Anglican Church (the Church of England).

Thomas Gallaudet

The French American educator Thomas Gallaudet (1787–1851) founded the first U.S. school for the deaf in Hartford, Connecticut, in 1817. Gallaudet studied European methods of instruction for those unable to hear or speak and modeled his school on the National Institute for the Deaf in Paris. He promoted advanced education for women and trained teachers who started schools for the deaf in other parts of the country. Gallaudet's son, Edward Gallaudet (1837–1917), founded one such school, now called Gallaudet University, near Washington, D.C.

The 17th-century French missionary and explorer Jacques Marquette, also known as Père Marquette, preaching to Native Americans. As well as being one of the first Europeans to explore the Mississippi River, Marquette was a Jesuit priest who set up several missions to bring Christianity to Native Americans.

The Wars of the 18th Century

In 1755 the British in Nova Scotia deported thousands of Acadian French (French immigrants to Acadia in Canada) who would not swear allegiance to them. The Acadians traveled to Louisiana, among other places, where they became known as Cajuns (a corruption of "Acadian"). In 1763 the war between England and France, known as the French and Indian War, ended. Under the Treaty of Paris, France surrendered part of its vast North American holdings in exchange for the return of former French territories in other parts of the world. The British gained Canada and all French lands east of the Mississippi except New Orleans and western Louisiana, which went to Spain. In 1803, the Americans bought the western Mississippi basin from the French in the Louisiana Purchase, pushing a large section of the American frontier west to the Rocky Mountains.

Despite relinquishing its political standing in America, France gave the American colonies invaluable support during the American Revolution of 1775, with 44,000 French troops serving in combat against the British armies. Many historians believe that without the direct involvement and assistance of the French, the United States would not have been formed.

Shortly afterward, in 1789, the French Revolution began in France. At its outbreak French Catholics sought refuge in the United States. Many wealthy aristocrats, or *bourgeoisie*, who were the target of the revolution, sought refuge along with the French working classes who were employed by the elite. These aristocrats settled largely in the urban areas of New York, Boston, Charleston, and New Orleans. During the same period 100 Catholic priests also left France for the United States. Since there were only 25 priests in America at the time, the French greatly influenced the formation of the American Catholic

John James Audubon

America's premier naturalist, John James Audubon (1785–1851) was the illegitimate son of a French sea captain who fought in the American Revolution. Audubon came to America at age 18 and spent his time hunting and drawing birds. He then devoted years to painting a catalog of every bird species in America. In 1826 he commissioned Robert Havell in London, England, to make copperplate engravings of his paintings. The resulting work, *Birds of America*, took 11 years to publish (1827–1838), and consisted of colored life-size plates of 1,065 birds. In 1866 the National Audubon Society, dedicated to the conservation of birds in America, was founded in his honor.

Church. French refugees, many of whom were political refugees, continued to arrive throughout the revolution, often emigrating to the United States via French colonies in the Caribbean.

Other French Immigrant Groups

In the 19th and 20th centuries several other significant waves of immigrants arrived from France. Some 30,000 French flocked to California during the Gold Rush from 1848 until 1851. Of these, 20,000, a record number, arrived in 1851. Largely unsuccessful in their endeavors to find gold, many remained in California and planted vineyards that helped establish the California wine country. French immigrants also arrived in America during the Franco–Prussian War of 1871, when the French provinces of Alsace and Lorraine came under German rule. During World War II (1939–1945), when the Germans occupied France in 1940, a significant number of French Jews and French intellectuals emigrated to the United States. Unlike the Jews, the intellectuals tended to return to France after the war.

Octave Chanute

Born in Paris, civil engineer Octave Chanute (1832–1910) came to the United States at age six. Chanute's interest in engineering led him to work on the railroads. As chief engineer of the Chicago and Alton Railroad, he designed Kansas City's Hannibal Bridge, the first bridge across the Missouri River. Chanute helped design the early elevated train system in New York City and became deeply involved in the aeronautical experiments of the day. His glider experiments in 1896 produced the Chanute Herring biplane glider, which later formed the basis of the Wright Brothers' biplane design.

The Successful French American Immigrant

French Americans have distinguished themselves in North America as successful entrepreneurs who have had a lasting impact on American society. They have been mostly middle-income, urban, and progressive. The Huguenots, for example, introduced skilled crafts such as lace making, silk making, and felt manufacture to North America. They also made modifications to the rice industry in South Carolina and became some of the wealthiest rice planters in the state. In addition, French-born bishops headed a number of newly created dioceses in the 19th century. Many French priests went to work in parishes in northern New England that had been set up by French immigrants from Quebec who settled in the region in the mid- to late 19th century to work in the mills.

Overall, the number of French who have come to North America is relatively low. However, if French immigration has been slow, it has also been stable over a long period of time, ranging from a high of 77,000 a year during the 1840s to a low of 18,000 during the 1970s. Not all the immigrants have arrived directly from France, however, since many have come via Canada or the Caribbean. Aside from the examples above, the French have mostly come to North America as individuals for

A street lined with bars and jazz saloons in the French quarter of New Orleans, Louisiana. The city is famous for its rich mix of cultures, particularly those of French and black origin.

Some popular American foods that reflect the influence of French cuisine, including croissants, French bread, pâté, and saucisson *(sausage).*

various personal reasons. They have tended to spread out geographically to areas of new opportunity, rather than settling in established immigrant communities. Some believe that the relatively humane and prosperous nature of France has made its people less likely to leave. In fact, in relation to the size of its population, France has taken in as many immigrants as the United States. The French who continued to settle in North America in the 19th and 20th centuries came in search of new opportunities. In the late 20th century, for example, many settled in California and the Southern "sun belt" states as the economy in that region prospered.

French Americans maintain an active interest in current events in France. In addition, they often return home. In the 1970s, for example, only one-third of the registered French immigrants eventually became American citizens. Since many of the French are middle-income, they can afford to go home, and their skills will often help them find work there.

Assimilation

French Americans have assimilated well into North American society. The trend of assimilation begun by the Huguenots continued with subsequent immigrants. French immigrants have been urban and middle-income, easily settling into cities where they blended in with American society. Many have been professionals attracted by the opportunities to be found in North America. They appear to have been as eager to innovate as to maintain national traditions. The French also have the highest rate of marriage outside of their ethnic group of any non-English speaking group in North America. Some historians point to an absence of group spirit among French Americans, which they attribute to a lack of French communities in North America and a general distaste among the French for group organization.

Jacques Cousteau

Born in France, Jacques Cousteau (1910–1997) served in the French Resistance during World War II and became a highly decorated naval officer. He helped invent the aqualung diving apparatus in 1943 and made his first underwater film while commanding the oceanographic research ship *Calypso* in the early 1950s. Cousteau developed an underwater television camera and made many films. His TV series *The Undersea World of Jacques Cousteau* (1968–1976) helped popularize marine biology. He also won an Academy Award for his documentary film *The Silent World* in 1957.

The Popularity of French Culture

The interest in French culture first began in the years after the American Revolution, but this is not due to any culture specifically maintained by French immigrants. Instead, America has looked to the French as cultural trendsetters. In part this influence results from the fact that many French settlers were aristocratic or wealthy, so their taste in clothes, food, furnishings, and paintings came to signify prosperity and success. As a language, French has been quite popular in America, particularly with the upper classes. Many French words have crept into English usage, such as automobile, garage, lingerie, bouquet, boutique, and croquet. Many Americans also studied French literature, music, and drama. The work of the French Impressionist painters of the late 19th and early 20th centuries also greatly influenced American art and taste.

Cuisine and Fashion

The French have in large part been responsible for an improvement in American cooking. The Huguenots first introduced yeast bread and rolls to North America, and were also the first to plant artichokes and tomatoes. Americans became enamored with French cuisine, and in the 19th century a French chef in Boston, known as Julien, became famous for his soups, consommés, and the introduction of the cheese omelet. French chefs and restaurants grew in number and popularity for years. Today, celebrity chefs such as Emeril Lagasse, who specializes in New Orleans cuisine, and Julia Child, who wrote *Mastering the Art of French Cooking*, demonstrate their cooking on popular American TV shows.

The American appetite for French fashion began in the early 19th century, partly due to the immigration of the hairdressers, dress designers, and perfumers who accompanied the exodus of French aristocrats during the French Revolution. The French introduced North Americans to such items as lace and gloves. Today Americans look to France as a leader in world fashion.

Revelers in the Mardi Gras street parade in New Orleans. With its exuberant costumes, floats, and merrymaking, it is one of the most flamboyant festivals in North America.

Folk Customs

Folklorists have found a few lingering French customs among older communities in the Midwest. In Michigan and parts of Appalachia the French custom of *charivari* (or *shivaree*), when neighbors make noise with pots and pans outside newlyweds' homes, still continues. Originally the noise was a sign of community disapproval of a marriage, for example, if one spouse was not Catholic or was recently bereaved. Today it is simply a prank played by friends on the new couple.

American square dancing also owes much of its form to an older style of French dancing called the *quadrille*, even though the dance was brought to North America with the English. French influence can be heard in dance calls such as "alemande" and "do-si-do."

Perhaps the best-known French custom in North America today is Mardi Gras, a raucous celebration that takes place each year in New Orleans the week before the beginning of Lent. Mardi Gras, literally "Fat Tuesday," is a huge street festival with parades, floats, and zany costumes. It has a long history and grew out of masked balls held by early French settlers. The occasion was first officially celebrated in New Orleans by a group of French American students in 1827.

See also

- Cajuns and Acadians (Volume 2)
- Canadians, French (Volume 2)
- Caribbean peoples (Volume 2)
- French Guyanese (Volume 4)
- Métis (Volume 7)
- Quebec separatism (Volume 9)

French Guyanese

Festivals

French Guyanese people follow French traditions and celebrate Bastille Day (July 14). In addition, one of the highlights of the calendar is Carnival, usually held in late February. An occasion for parades, dancing, and feasting, Carnival in French Guyana combines traditional Caribbean exuberance with European style.

See also

- Caribbean peoples (Volume 2)
- Festivals (Volume 4)
- French (Volume 4)
- Guyanese (Volume 4)

Slightly smaller than the state of Indiana, French Guyana is the only French-speaking country in South America. In 1946 it was made a *département* of France and sends two elected representatives to the National Assembly and one to the Senate in Paris. Its education and welfare systems are based on those in France.

Since it is technically part of France, no separate data about French Guyanese migration to the United States exists. From the ethnically diverse population of 178,000, about 1,700 migrate each year, but their destination is unknown. Many go to France, where they have the right to live and work and where they can speak the language.

As much as 80 percent of French Guyana is covered in forest and is virtually uninhabitable. The forest provides valuable export commodities, in addition to the other export industries of agriculture and fishing. Despite having the highest standard of living in South America, French Guyana imports much more than it exports. France and the United States are major trading partners, and the economy largely survives due to French subsidies. Most French Guyanese are of mixed race, but there are also people who are ethnically Indian, Chinese, and Middle Eastern, as well as those from other French colonies. In recent years French Guyana has admitted immigrants from Laos, Vietnam, Haiti, and the French Caribbean islands.

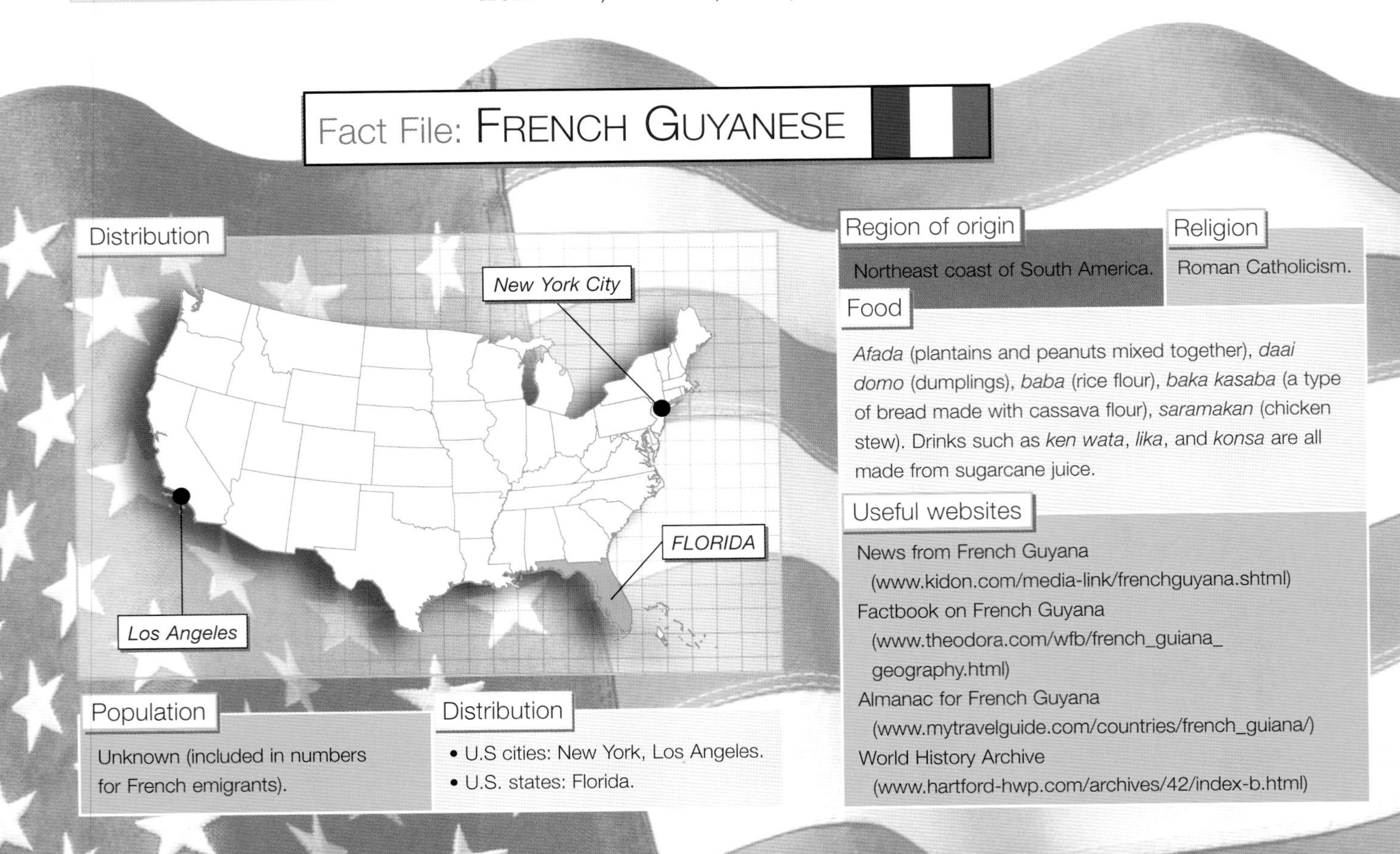

Fact File: French Guyanese

Distribution

Population

Unknown (included in numbers for French emigrants).

Distribution

- U.S cities: New York, Los Angeles.
- U.S. states: Florida.

Region of origin

Northeast coast of South America.

Religion

Roman Catholicism.

Food

Afada (plantains and peanuts mixed together), *daai domo* (dumplings), *baba* (rice flour), *baka kasaba* (a type of bread made with cassava flour), *saramakan* (chicken stew). Drinks such as *ken wata*, *lika*, and *konsa* are all made from sugarcane juice.

Useful websites

News from French Guyana
(www.kidon.com/media-link/frenchguyana.shtml)
Factbook on French Guyana
(www.theodora.com/wfb/french_guiana_geography.html)
Almanac for French Guyana
(www.mytravelguide.com/countries/french_guiana/)
World History Archive
(www.hartford-hwp.com/archives/42/index-b.html)

Frontier

The American frontier is the name given to the region that formed the edge of immigrant-settled or "developed" territory in North America. Inside what is now the United States, the frontier moved north from Mexico, west from the Atlantic, and southeast across the Bering Strait into Alaska, all between the 16th and early 20th centuries. It was shaped by the desire of European colonists for farmland and natural resources, and by their relationship with, and subsequent domination of, the Native American peoples who already lived on the continent. Always in a state of flux, the frontier affected different regions at different times until the entire continent was settled by immigrants and their descendants at end of the 19th and beginning of the 20th centuries.

Pioneers of the American Frontier

Early Spanish settlers came to Florida and New Mexico in the 1500s. Other European explorers, fur traders, and missionaries arrived on the continent in the 16th and 17th centuries. In the 1600s Samuel de Champlain and the French *voyageurs*, sometimes accompanied by Jesuit priests, established a vast fur-trading empire throughout the Great Lakes. They relied on intensive trade with Hurons and other Native Americans to trap the beaver that they exported to Europe. When the Dutch claimed the New Netherlands in the early 17th century, they too traded for furs, which were provided by the Iroquois. English settlers, many of whom were Protestant, were also attracted by the fur trade. They quickly turned to farming and transatlantic trade in a variety of natural resources derived from their settlements that stretched from New England down the coast to Georgia. This pushed the frontier west to the Appalachians. In the southeast, however, English and Scots settlers competed on an international frontier with the Spanish and French in the profitable deer-hide trade that relied on the hunting skills of the Creek, Cherokee, Choctaw, and Chickasaw.

In the 18th century several different waves of European immigrants, along with Africans brought over in the slave trade, flowed into North America. Many Europeans wanted land, while others, such as the Amish who arrived in Pennsylvania in the 1720s, sought freedom from religious persecution. To serve the new immigrants after the Revolution, the young American government negotiated over 700 treaties with Native American nations. However, immigrants on the frontier often moved onto native lands before any negotiations had taken place, leading to recurrent warfare.

Manifest Destiny

This term encapsulated the American belief that the United States had been entrusted with a special mission by God to spread its political and moral values and support its rising population by taking control of the largely unsettled territories west of the Mississippi River. "Manifest Destiny" was a phrase first used in 1845 by John L. Sullivan, a writer who championed the rights of Americans "to overspread the continent allotted by Providence for the free development of our yearly multiplying millions." It was an idea that underpinned the westward expansion of the United States for the following 50 years.

A wagon train of American homesteaders migrating to the West moves across the open plains in this photograph taken in 1885.

American explorers Meriwether Lewis (1774–1809) and William Clark (1770–1838) at the mouth of the Columbia River in 1805. The Lewis and Clark expedition (1804–1806) was ordered by President Thomas Jefferson to explore the territory westward from Louisiana. Lewis and Clark traveled a total of 8,000 miles (12,800km) and became the first whites to cross North America within what is now the United States. Their expedition greatly increased knowledge of the West and opened the way for the millions that would follow throughout the 19th century.

See also

- Colonial America (Volume 3)
- English (Volume 4)
- French (Volume 4)
- Native Americans (Volumes 7 & 8)
- Spanish (Volume 10)

Displacing Native American Peoples

By the 1820s the expansion of colonial cotton farms along the Gulf of Mexico and wheat and livestock farms in the Midwest threatened to surround the remaining native nations of these regions. The United States reacted by passing the Indian Removal Act of 1830, which forced more than 50,000 eastern Native Americans to move from their traditional homelands to designated "Indian Territory." In Alaska Russian fur traders overran Aleut communities but failed to dislodge the Tlingit of southeast Alaska. In New Mexico and, later, California the native and Spanish/Mexican frontier was molded by Franciscan missionaries, native military revolts, and the deadly impact of European disease, which historians believe destroyed up to 90 percent of the Native American population during the frontier era.

The Western Frontier

In the early 19th century Americans who had lived largely in the East began to look west to the lands that lay beyond the Mississippi River. Paced by government expeditions, explorers like Meriwether Lewis and William Clark opened up new areas of the continent to European settlers, and their achievements have been mythologized by writers and filmmakers ever since. Less well known are the "mountain men," like Jedediah Smith, who lived among the Native Americans. They used their knowledge to guide emigrants along the Oregon Trail and California cutoff, routes that attracted half a million Americans between the 1840s and the 1860s.

Among these immigrants were thousands of Scots, Irish, Scandinavians, and Germans, who pushed the frontier toward the Pacific and then followed it as it pulsed east again, pursuing gold and silver discoveries in California, Nevada, and Colorado. The Mormon exodus illustrates the rapid westward movement of the 19th century. Seeking religious asylum, they journeyed west from Illinois into Deseret, the future Utah, where they founded Salt Lake City in 1847. Chinese and Irish laborers were employed to build the first transcontinental railroad, completed in 1869, exemplifying the variety of people who shaped the frontier of the Great Plains, Rocky Mountains, and Pacific West.

In the decades following the Civil War (1861–65) the railroad brought immigrants West and shipped cattle, wheat, timber, and other natural resources back to the East. However, the hey-day of the cattle industry and wheat farms that flourished in the Great Plains directly after the war was over by 1890. That year also marked the defeat of the Lakota people at Wounded Knee Creek, South Dakota, signaling the military defeat of Native Americans in the West. In 1893 Frederick Jackson Turner, a young historian from the University of Wisconsin, announced the "End of the Frontier."

Georgians

Ethnic Georgians originated from the territory of present-day Georgia, which borders Russia, Turkey, Armenia, and Azerbaijan. Throughout history the region has experienced invasion from each of the Ottoman, Persian, and Russian empires. Georgia itself was divided between Ottoman and Persian spheres of influence in the early 16th century. In the 18th century the Ottoman Empire became increasingly influential before Russia officially annexed Georgia in 1801. After a brief period of independence between 1918 and 1921 Georgia was incorporated into the Soviet Union, which was ruled from 1929 to 1953 by the Georgian-born dictator Joseph Stalin. On April 9, 1991, Georgia declared independence and became a sovereign state. Despite a history of repeated invasion, Georgians have been able to maintain their distinct culture and traditions.

History of Immigration

The history of Georgian immigration to North America is not well documented. Unlike other ethnic groups, Georgians are not listed independently in the U.S. or Canadian censuses. Since 1990 the U.S. State Department has actively tracked emigration from Georgia. The task is complex because many Georgians leave their homeland for one or more years and then return, while others settle permanently in other countries. According to State Department data, approximately 218,800 of Georgia's 5.4 million population emigrated between 1990 and 1997. Other estimates place this number at 1,077,000, or 20 percent of Georgia's population. Such large numbers of emigrants have posed significant problems for the country.

As a result of Georgia's poor economic conditions, many Georgians have emigrated to North America since 1991 to find work and send their paychecks back to their families. Statistics suggest that the majority of these well-educated individuals, many of whom hold college degrees, will ultimately return to Georgia. This is particularly true since U.S. work visas are difficult for Georgian citizens to acquire.

Emigration from Georgia has occurred for political reasons at other times during the 20th century. For example, Georgians fled to the West in 1921 following the Soviet occupation of their country. Another wave of immigration began in 1924 following an unsuccessful Georgian uprising against the Soviet Red Army. As a result of this defeat, approximately 5,000 Georgians were executed, and more than 100,000 were exiled to Siberia under the Stalinist system. Several Georgians who fled the country in 1921 and 1924

George Balanchine

George Balanchine was a world-renowned ballet choreographer. Born in the Caucasus region of Georgia in 1904, he moved to Russia at the age of nine in order to study dance at the St. Petersburg Academy. In 1933 he moved to the United States, and in 1934 he founded the School of American Ballet. In 1946 he helped form the Ballet Society. When the New York City Ballet was created in 1948, Balanchine (below left) became its first artistic director, a position he held until his death in 1983.

founded the Georgian Association in the United States of America in 1932. This nationwide organization continues to represent Georgian interests in the United States today.

Georgian Culture Today

While the founders of the Georgian Association in the United States were dedicated to promoting future Georgian independence, the organization has since become a source of information about Georgian culture, politics, and activities. The association publishes a quarterly newsletter and a website, and helps provide educational opportunities for ethnic Georgians, in particular with regard to preserving the distinctive Georgian language.

As Georgia continues its struggle toward democracy and a market economy, efforts are being made to promote cooperation with Georgian communities outside the republic. For example, the American-Georgian Business Council has been established to increase economic ties between the United States and Georgia. As economic and political stability began to improve in Georgia in the second half of the 1990s, migration decreased. It is still unclear, however, how many Georgians in North America will remain and how many will return to Georgia in order to help rebuild their country.

See also

- Armenians (Volume 1)
- Azerbaijanis (Volume 1)
- Central Asians (Volume 2)
- Russians (Volume 9)
- Turks (Volume 10)

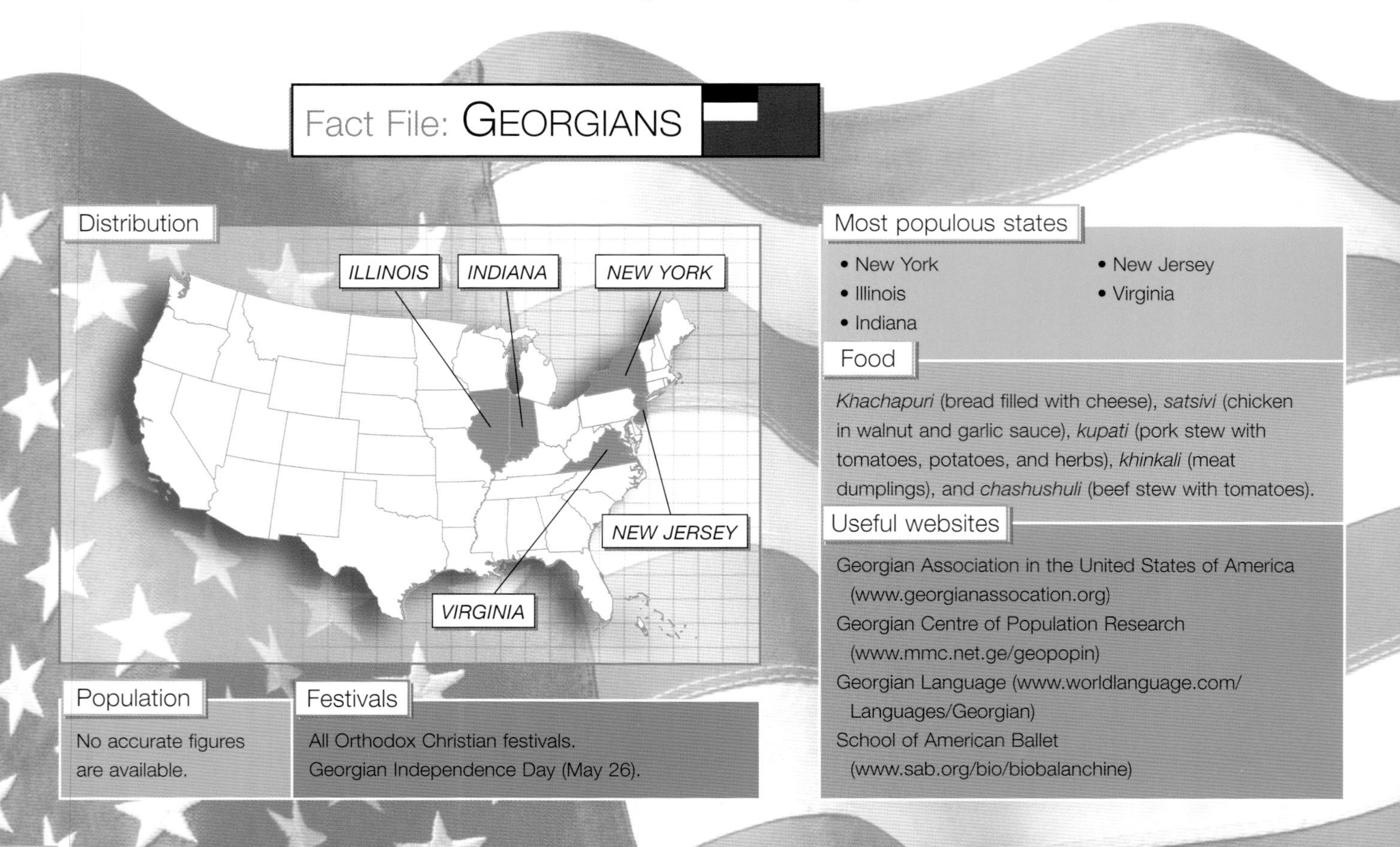

Population

No accurate figures are available.

Festivals

All Orthodox Christian festivals.
Georgian Independence Day (May 26).

Most populous states

- New York
- Illinois
- Indiana
- New Jersey
- Virginia

Food

Khachapuri (bread filled with cheese), *satsivi* (chicken in walnut and garlic sauce), *kupati* (pork stew with tomatoes, potatoes, and herbs), *khinkali* (meat dumplings), and *chashushuli* (beef stew with tomatoes).

Useful websites

Georgian Association in the United States of America (www.georgianassocation.org)
Georgian Centre of Population Research (www.mmc.net.ge/geopopin)
Georgian Language (www.worldlanguage.com/Languages/Georgian)
School of American Ballet (www.sab.org/bio/biobalanchine)

Germans

German peoples are counted among the first, largest, and most successful groups of Europeans to settle in North America. Over a span of about 400 years their descendants have swelled in number to tens of millions, and many of their customs, traditions, and ideas have become part of the mainstream American and Canadian cultures. While their original settlements were concentrated on the northeast coast of what is now the United States, today large numbers live throughout America and Canada. They are found in every occupation and walk of life. Currently there are 32 million Americans and 2.5 million Canadians claiming German ancestry.

German-speaking peoples have come to North America not only from Germany but also from many other countries, including Austria, Switzerland, Poland, Luxembourg, and Russia. Some came to escape religious or political persecution in their homeland, while others came hoping to improve their standard of living.

Waves of Immigration

The millions of German artisans, laborers, farmers, scholars, political activists, and others who came during the peak period of German immigration, from the late 1600s until the late 1800s, played a significant role in building the fledgling United States and Canada. They cleared and settled land, helped build towns and cities, and set up new industries. In the 20th century other groups of Germans made North America their home to escape the turmoil and destruction surrounding World War I (1914–1918) and World War II (1939–1945), and the subsequent division of Germany into two separate countries: East Germany and West Germany.

Assimilation

The majority of Americans and Canadians of German heritage have assimilated so successfully over the centuries that it is difficult now to distinguish them. Some observe German traditions and holidays, however, with special parades, festivals, and other cultural events.

Useful websites

Society for German-American Studies, Indiana University-Purdue University Indianapolis (www-lib.iupui.edu/kade)
German-American Chamber of Commerce (www.gaccwest.org)
German-American National Congress (www.dank.org)
German-American Heritage Center (www.germanamerheritage.org)

Albert Einstein

The famous scientist Albert Einstein (1879–1955) was a German Jew who emigrated to the United States in 1933 following the Nazi rise to power in Germany. He is shown below taking the oath of U.S. citizenship with his secretary Helen Dukas (left) and his daughter Margaret (right). Before his move Einstein enjoyed a brilliant career in physics and won the Nobel Prize (1921) for his work. In later life he was an outspoken peace activist.

Fact File: GERMANS

Distribution

People of German ancestry live in virtually every state, province, and city of the United States and Canada. The largest concentrations of German Americans are found in Pennsylvania, New York, Ohio, Wisconsin, Illinois, Minnesota, Iowa, Missouri, Nebraska, Kansas, California, and Texas.
Most German Canadians live in Ontario, Alberta, British Columbia, Saskatchewan, and Manitoba.

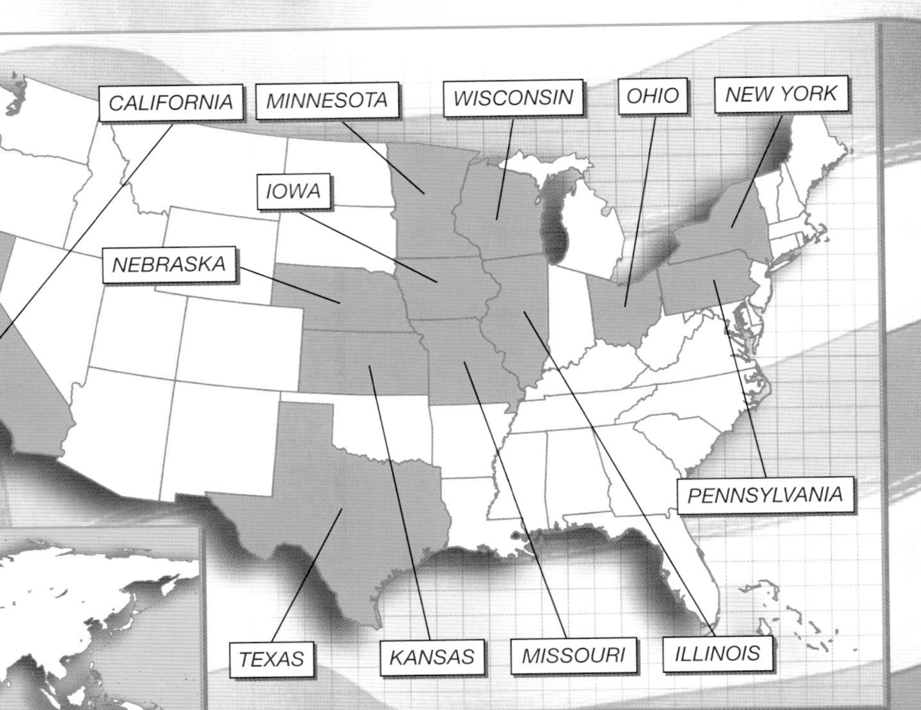

Region of origin

German-speaking immigrants have come to North America from Germany, as well as Austria, Switzerland, Poland, Luxembourg, and Russia.

Population

- United States (2000 census): 32,529,108.
- Canada (1996 census): 2,757,140.

Language

The majority of German descendants speak English as their first language. In addition to English some speak one of several dialects of German, which belongs to the Indo-European family of languages.

Dates of major arrivals

- Late 1600s through the late 1800s.
- 1919–1939.
- 1945–1970.

Jobs

German Americans and Canadians occupy every profession. Early immigrants were farmers, tradespeople, and laborers.

First immigrants

German artisans arrived on October 1, 1608, to help British settlers in founding Jamestown, Virginia.

Names

Several signs identify a name of likely German origin, including:
- The letters "sch" at the name's beginning, as in Schafer, Schmidt, Schneider, Schultz, and Schwartz;
- The letters "ei," as in Eisenhower, Reichmann, Klein, and Weiss;
- The endings -mann, -burg, -berg, -lich, -stein, or -t(h)al.

Food

Hamburgers, schnitzels (breaded veal or pork), sauerkraut (shredded and pickled cabbage), and sausages including wieners (made from smoked beef or pork).

Religion

Christianity, mainly Protestantism, but some Roman Catholicism. Also Judaism.

Festivals

Most major festivals are based on Christian or Jewish holidays. Others include:
Steuben Parades: held in New York, Chicago, and Philadelphia (September) to honor Baron Friedrich Wilhelm von Steuben, who helped train George Washington's troops during the Revolutionary War.
German American Day in the United States (October 6).
Oktoberfest (October), which has its origins in a fair held to celebrate the marriage of the Bavarian prince Ludwig to Princess Thérèse of Saxe-Hildburghausen in 1810.

Germany's reunification in 1990, after 45 years of occupation and separation following World War II, was cause for celebration among German Americans and Canadians.

Early German Immigrants

Many centuries ago German lands covered a large part of Europe, stretching from the North and Baltic seas to the Alps Mountains, and from the Rhine River east into present-day Russia. These lands were divided into hundreds of small states, each with its own ruler. The largest states included Prussia, Bavaria, Saxony, and Austria. United in name as the Holy Roman Empire, in reality these states often competed against one another in politics and war.

Protestantism, a new kind of Christianity inspired by the German priest Martin Luther (1483–1546), further divided the German states after the 16th century. The states that converted to Protestantism fought against those that remained Roman Catholic in the Thirty Years' War (1618–1648), one of Europe's most devastating conflicts. Even after peace was declared, religious intolerance was widespread.

In 1608 a few German artisans helped the British establish their first permanent settlement in North America, called Jamestown, in Virginia. Their valuable skills helped the new colony grow. In the following decades more Germans were offered work in Jamestown as well as other new settlements.

Germans began arriving in larger numbers by the end of the 1600s. Most were not looking for jobs, but were escaping from religious persecution in their homelands. William Penn of England, a Quaker, imagined building a community in North America where Quakers could worship freely. In 1681 he founded the colony of Pennsylvania. In 1683 German Quakers founded Germantown, Pennsylvania, the first German settlement in North America.

Germantown's success encouraged more German immigration. People came to escape religious persecution or to improve their standard of living. Over the next two centuries millions of Germans came to the United States and Canada. Their numbers peaked in the last half of the 1800s, at a time of overpopulation and war in Europe.

Concord School House, built in 1775 in Germantown, Pennsylvania. Germantown was the first German settlement in North America, and schools and churches provided focal points for the new community.

The "48ers"

Revolutions rocked Europe in 1848, as citizens tried to overthrow their monarchs and establish democratic governments in which leaders were elected. In German lands the revolutionaries were unsuccessful and soon had to flee for fear of arrest or execution. About 10,000 of them fled to the United States. Many were outstanding scholars and political activists who devoted their talents to causes in America.

The immigrants went to both established settlements and the frontier. Farmers settled in the countryside, while artisans and laborers moved to towns and cities.

In Europe German states united to form the new country of Germany in 1871. As Germany prospered, emigration to the United States slowed. The next large group, tens of thousands of Volga or Black Sea Germans, came from Russia to escape religious persecution from the 1860s onward. The 20th century also witnessed several major waves of German emigration. The aftermath of World War I brought severe economic and political upheaval to Germany, which in turn led to the rise of Adolf Hitler's violent and racist Nazi government in 1933. Over a half-million Germans left their country for North America during this period, 100,000 of them Jews. The final wave of German immigrants came after 1945, seeking new opportunities because of the physical devastation suffered by Germany in World War II. During the 1950s and 1960s German immigration continued, with over 750,000 Germans moving to the United States in search of a better standard of living.

German Jews

The 100,000 German Jews who immigrated to North America from the 1930s onward settled mostly in large cities, where they made themselves at home among previously settled Jewish communities. Many of these new immigrants were talented scientists, scholars, and artists who throughout their lives made important contributions to the United States and Canada.

German Communities in North America

The 13 Quaker families who founded Germantown created a remarkably close-knit community. By building homes together in a village and keeping their farmland on the outskirts of town, they strengthened bonds between neighbors. People cooperated in daily activities, which were structured around a strict routine of worship and hard work. As they prospered, residents started several small industries, including weaving, woodworking, leather tanning, and printing, that helped supply the nearby city of Philadelphia. Their success paved the way for future German migrants.

Despite the high cost of tickets for places on sailing ships that crossed the Atlantic Ocean to the United States, Germans came steadily throughout the 1700s. Those who could not afford to pay their way often came as "redemptioners." In exchange for paid passage to North America they signed a contract for four to seven years' hard work as the servant of a farmer, business owner, or other employer on their arrival. Many "redemptioners," once they had fulfilled the terms of their contract, worked to save enough money to pay for their family's passage across the Atlantic so that they could be reunited.

German emigrants bound for North America boarding a steam ship in Hamburg, Germany, in 1874.

By the 1800s Germans and their descendants were a dominant group in North America and began to have an impact on politics. On the whole, they were opposed to slavery, and they were also instrumental in electing Abraham Lincoln as president in 1861. German tradespeople and craftspeople brought with them from Europe the guild system, in which organizations called guilds regulated the training and quality of craftsmanship and protected their members' trading rights. The guild system played an important role in the creation of U.S. trade unions in the last half of the 19th century.

The Philippus Kirche in Cincinnati, Ohio, which dates from the end of the 19th century. Its tall, narrow shape, pointed spire, and large hall inside are typical of German Protestant churches built in the United States and elsewhere.

Despite their contributions, German immigrants and their descendants became targets of hatred during World War I. Violence toward and prejudice against anything German prompted many people of German descent to distance themselves from their heritage and assimilate as much as possible. Although present, anti-German sentiment was not so strong during World War II, in part because of the strong opposition among German Americans and Canadians to the Nazi government in their homeland.

Germans in Mainstream America

Today the descendants of German immigrants are part of mainstream society more than ever before. German Americans and Canadians can be found in all professions and at all income levels. They have held the American presidency and Canadian prime ministership. They have also partnered and had children with people from most other ethnic backgrounds. Their diverse family structures and homes reflect those of other North Americans.

The 1990 U.S. census showed that families of German descent have an average income of $38,216, placing them in the middle range of earners in the United States. The census also confirmed that they are generally well educated, with 83 percent in the United States having graduated high school and 22 percent having completed a bachelor's degree or higher.

In the case of German Americans and Canadians assimilation has not meant the complete abandonment of traditional language, culture, and values, some of which have shaped mainstream culture. In recent decades various organizations have worked to celebrate German descendants' ethnic identities. German-style parades, festivals, and other events are organized each year in communities across the continent.

The least assimilated German descendants are known as the "Pennsylvania Dutch" ("Dutch" coming from "Deutsch," meaning German). They live in their own communities and dedicate

Pennsylvania Dutch

The "Pennsylvania Dutch," also known as the "Pennsylvania Germans," are the religious communities of Quakers, Amish, Moravians, Dunkers, Mennonites, and Hutterites who live in the Pennsylvania region. They are in fact German, not Dutch. The term "Dutch" is an Americanization of the German word "Deutsch" (meaning "German"). Today the Pennsylvania Dutch continue practices such as sharing money and property with their community, abstaining from military service, and following a strict daily routine centered around Christian worship. They are best known outside their communities for their skill as farmers and artisans, as well as for preserving a centuries-old way of life.

themselves to religious beliefs that value hard physical labor, traditional clothing, and the rejection of most modern conveniences. Many continue speaking German and in most other ways live as the founders of Germantown lived centuries ago.

Notable German Americans

John Jacob Astor, billionaire.
Marlene Dietrich, actress.
John D. Diefenbaker, Canadian prime minister (1957–1963).
Albert Einstein, scientist.
Dwight D. Eisenhower, U.S. president (1953–1961).
Walter Gropius, architect.
Henry Kissinger, U.S. secretary of state.
Mies van der Rohe, architect.
Charles M. Schultz, cartoonist.
Theodore Seuss Geisel, *Dr. Seuss* author and illustrator.
Levi Strauss, inventor of jeans.

Arts and Culture

German immigrants brought with them a wide range of traditions. However, the image most North Americans have of German culture is that from the city of Munich in Bavaria, southern Germany. Bavarian costume, which includes leather shorts and suspenders called lederhosen and hats with feathers, is often worn by German marching bands and dancers in parades.

Such cultural events usually observe a Christian holiday, like Christmas, or one celebrating German achievement, such as the Steuben Day parades in New York, Chicago, and Philadelphia each September. They honor Baron Friedrich von Steuben (1730–1794), who helped train George Washington's troops during the American Revolutionary War. The most famous German contribution to holidays in North America is the Christmas tree, which was said to have been introduced in Germany by Martin Luther.

The vast majority of immigrants were members of the Reformed or Lutheran Churches, two denominations of Protestant Christianity. There were also many Roman Catholics. While some of their descendants have continued to follow these churches, others have converted to other denominations or joined in the mainstream trend toward a decline in religious observance.

Oktoberfest

Oktoberfest is a traditional two-week festival celebrated in the south German city of Munich. It has its origins in a fair held to celebrate the marriage of the Bavarian prince Ludwig to Princess Thérèse of Saxe-Hildburghausen in 1810. Crowds parade and gather in tents and halls to drink beer, play and listen to music, sing, and dance. This boisterous festival is also marked in North America, notably in the Canadian city of Kitchener-Waterloo, Ontario, which is home to a large German community.

German films, music, and writing have had a major influence on North American arts in the 20th century. Thousands of intellectuals, writers, artists, actors, and musicians immigrated in the 1930s to escape Nazi terror in Hitler's Germany. They included the actress Marlene Dietrich, the composer Kurt Weill, and the writer Thomas Mann.

German foods have also gained great popularity. They include Hamburger steaks (hamburgers) and frankfurter sausages (hot dogs), both named after the cities in Germany from which they originally came. German ketchup and pickles were popularized by the German American Henry John Heinz. Milton Hershey, another German American, invented the chocolate bar. The North American beer industry has also been dominated by German names, including Anheuser-Busch, Schlitz, and Coors.

Henry Kissinger was born in Germany in 1923 and fled to the United States with his family in 1938 to escape the Nazi persecution of Jews. He became an influential authority on international affairs and defense, and played a key role in U.S. foreign policy in the 1960s and 1970s. In 1968 he was made assistant to the president for national security affairs, in 1969 he became head of the National Security Council, and in 1973 he was appointed the 56th U.S. secretary of state.

Politics and the Home Country

It is not surprising that many Americans and Canadians of German ancestry feel no strong connection to Germany. Their ancestors may have immigrated hundreds of years ago, a span of time that has made European culture and politics a distant memory. Not everyone shares this indifference, however. In particular, the first, second, and third generations of Germans who have lived in North America since the 20th century often remain very much in touch with their homeland. In fact, Germany has been so central in world politics for the last century that it has been hard for them to escape its influence. They have watched as their country fought two world wars, followed by a painful division into East Germany—controlled by the Soviet Union—and West Germany, backed by the countries of western Europe, the United States, and Canada.

Following their opposition to Germany's Nazi government of the 1930s and 1940s, many German Americans and Canadians joined in opposition to the Soviet Union's control of East Germany. West Germany was protected by the United States and its allies many times after the war. Through the Marshall Plan (1948–1951) the United States also invested billions of dollars to rebuild West Germany and its industries. Opposition to Soviet control of East Germany grew after the East German government constructed the Berlin Wall in 1961, cutting off many people from their relatives. Following the fall of communism and the reunification of Germany in 1990, the United States has retained its good relations with Germany.

See also

- Amish (Volume 1)
- Cold War and ethnicity (Volume 2)
- Mennonites (Volume 7)
- Mormons (Volume 7)
- World War I (Volume 10)
- World War II (Volume 10)

Ghettos

Harlem

Harlem, in the upper Manhattan part of New York City, is one of America's most famous African American neighborhoods. Between 1920 and 1930 nearly 175,000 black Americans migrated to the 3-square-mile neighborhood in search of work, and a unique culture grew up there. Today Harlem is a more diverse community, including whites, Asians, and large numbers of Hispanics. The majority of the employed work as administrative secretaries, laborers, managerial professionals, hospital workers, and fast-food employees. However, Harlem remains an economically depressed area with substantial unemployment and poor housing.

The term "ghetto" is centuries old and was originally used to describe a quarter of a city in which Jews were forced to live. These districts were often enclosed by walls; and as houses were built and extended, they became very overcrowded. Ghettos were abolished in western Europe in the 19th century but remained in some countries until the mid-20th century. More recently the term has been used to describe any urban area exclusively settled by a minority group—often recent immigrants. It brings with it connotations of poverty, social deprivation, overcrowding, and crime, as well as associations of rich ethnic and cultural identities.

The location and make-up of ghettos change over time according to economic and social factors. As communities formerly associated with run-down urban areas become more financially secure, they often move out to wealthier suburbs, making way for new groups of immigrants. In the 20th century ghettos came to be most closely associated with black neighborhoods. However, from the late 19th century until the middle of the 20th century districts settled by poor Jewish, Italian, Irish, and Chinese communities were also considered ghettos. More recently, urban areas with large Hispanic and Native American populations have been similarly labeled.

Historical Overview

During several periods of North American history immigrants to the United States and Canada were poorer than native-born peoples. In the early part of the 20th century non-English-speaking European immigrants grouped together in their own communities to a higher degree than American-born people. In the urban areas to which they flocked in search of work, they rented rooms in tenements, high-density blocks of housing often built to low specifications. Tenements had poor sanitation, lighting, and heating, and soon became overcrowded. Substantial ghettos of non-English-speaking European immigrants largely disappeared following World War II, as assimilation with native whites became more common. However, many ghettos of black Americans that developed between 1910 and 1950, when 5.5 million black Americans migrated from the South in search of work, persist today, as do an increasing number of poor Hispanic neighborhoods. In the

A run-down street in Harlem, New York City, photographed in 1967. It is a stereotypical image of a ghetto. Communities of ethnic minorities in cities have often also produced rich and dynamic urban cultures.

20th century tenements gave way to public housing funded by federal and state governments. These "projects" house a disproportionate number of impoverished black and Hispanics.

Today black Americans stand out as the most disadvantaged group of people in the United States. The poverty rate for blacks, though at an all-time low in 2000, was almost three times that of whites, at 22.1 percent, according to census data. In 1995 roughly four times as many blacks and three times as many Hispanics—compared to whites—lived in "poverty areas," where more than 20 percent of residents were classified as poor by the U.S. government.

Ghetto Life

Families who live in urban poverty tend to be larger than those in wealthier areas. Sometimes extended family members such as grandparents, aunts, uncles, and cousins live under the same roof to save money, or because living together is a common practice for their particular ethnic group, as, for example, in Hispanic neighborhoods in Texas and California. In many poor, black neighborhoods households are headed by a single woman, either a mother, an aunt, or even an eldest child. Unstable family environments contribute to rising membership in gangs and social problems like crime.

Despite higher rates of crime and poverty, so-called "ghetto" neighborhoods often also produce unique, rich cultures. Community organizations like church groups, youth centers, and theater and art studios cultivate a sense of togetherness and help provide a sense of belonging. The Harlem Boys' Choir and the Harlem Girls' Choir, which serve African American youths in New York City, are outstanding examples.

Tackling Urban Segregation and Poverty

The problem of segregation in the urban population was brought to the fore by the Civil Rights Movement in the 1960s. The U.S. government introduced a number of measures to improve housing standards, including the 1968 Fair Housing Act, which sought to tackle discrimination in the housing market. Recently many government housing authorities, like that in Chicago, have begun to demolish high-rise public housing projects and to replace them with mixed-income developments and privately owned housing in order to integrate communities more fully. Despite government action, however, researchers have shown that many minorities, particularly black Americans, continue to face prejudice both in the housing market and more generally. Areas of urban deprivation populated by ethnic minorities remain a reality in American cities.

Deprived urban areas

Many of America's largest and most dynamic cities also include neighborhoods of extreme poverty. They are often the only places in which new immigrants and low-income or unemployed citizens can afford to live. Different ethnic and religious minorities often cluster together within them, living in multiunit rental housing. Some of the country's most disadvantaged city neighborhoods are as follows:

- New York: Harlem and Bedford-Stuyvesant (black with increasing numbers of Hispanic immigrants)
- Los Angeles: Watts (black) and the Barrio (Hispanic)
- Chicago: Westside and Southside (black).

Graffiti in San Francisco, California. Murals like this are some of the most visible forms of cultural expression in poor city areas.

See also

- Cities, U.S. (Volume 2)
- Crime, ethnic (Volume 3)
- Housing (Volume 5)
- Segregation and integration (Volume 9)

Greeks

The owner of a Greek coffeehouse in Aliquippa, Pennsylvania. Many Greek immigrants set up their own stores and restaurants.

Known for their hard work and entrepreneurial skills, and their emphasis on democracy, freedom, and education, Greek immigrants blended quickly into American culture in the first half of the 20th century. Though much Greek culture has been lost across the generations with rapid assimilation into mainstream American culture, recent immigrants and Greek American organizations work to maintain an ethnic identity. As one of the most highly educated segments of the U.S. population, Greek Americans hold high-level posts in public and private sectors.

Philanthropy

The word "philanthropy" comes from the Greek word *philanthropos*, which means "the love of human beings." A philanthropist nurtures the well-being of others by gathering donations for good causes or volunteers his or her time to those in need. Greeks, and Greek Americans, have a long history of philanthropy. The largest Greek American, nonreligious organization is the American Hellenic Educational Progressive Association (AHEPA). Founded in Atlanta, Georgia, in 1922 to help Greeks settle and become successful in America, the organization today is mainly philanthropic. Donations go toward fighting cancer, muscular dystrophy, anemia, and autism, to name a few. In addition, AHEPA sponsors athletes and students. It also expresses its opinions to the U.S. government in the interests of Greek–American relations.

History of Immigration

The first Greek to set foot on North American soil was John Griego, a Greek who lived in Genoa, Italy, and sailed with Christopher Columbus in 1492. Greeks did not begin emigrating to North America in large numbers until the 1890s, when Greece struggled with political and economic turmoil. Though the country had gained independence from the Ottoman Empire, a corrupt government followed. The poor were forced to pay between 10 and 40 percent of their income in taxes, while the ruling class paid no taxes at all.

In addition to high taxes Greek custom called for daughters to have dowries to accompany a marriage arrangement. Not to provide a dowry was dishonorable. Population increase also put pressure on the available farmland. These factors contributed to the decision of many Greeks to emigrate in search of better economic prospects. Many immigrants of the 1890s and 1910s intended to return home with savings.

In 1912 about 45,000 men returned to fight for Greece in the Balkan Wars against Turkey. Afterward most returned to America to start businesses. Greek women joined them and helped establish Greek Orthodox churches.

Since the early 20th century Greek arrivals fluctuated along with U.S. immigration laws. The 1965 Immigration Act, which gave preference to members of established families, spurred an influx of 140,000 Greeks between 1965 and 1975. This wave of immigration was also influenced by political unrest in Greece. After the country's slow return to stability following German occupation in World War II, Colonel George Papadopoulos staged a military coup in 1967 that resulted in an end to constitutional rights and the monarchy. His government was overthrown in 1973, and in 1974 Greece held its first democratic elections for 10 years.

Fact File: Greeks

Distribution

Most populous states:
- Illinois
- New York
- Maryland

Most populous cities:
- Chicago
- New York
- Baltimore

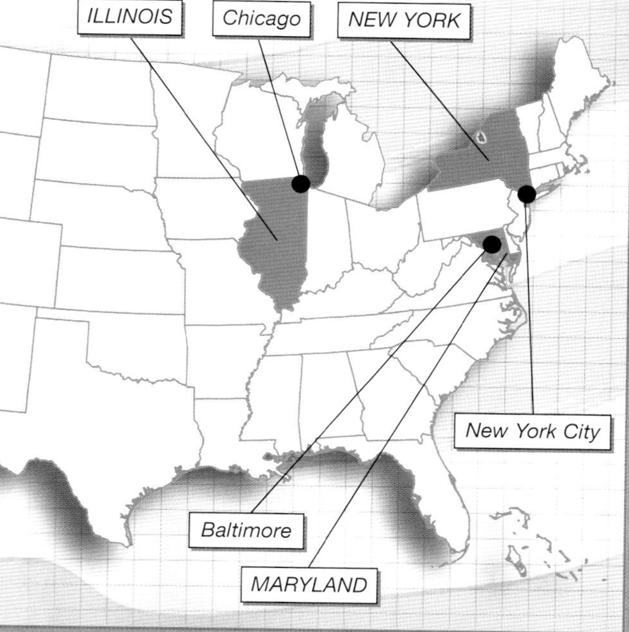

Region of origin

Greece is in the Mediterranean region of southern Europe.

Population

957,795 (2000 census).

Language

Greek and English.

Community organizations

American Hellenic Educational Progressive Association (www.AHEPA.org)

Socrates Greek American School, founded in 1907 as the first Greek School in North America. It offers bilingual education in Greek and English (www.socratesschool.org)

Greek American Folklore Association (www.hri.org/GAFS)

Useful websites

Greece Today
A daily news and information resource from Greece for professionals, students, and teachers (www.europeaninternet.com/greece)

History of Greek Dancing
(www.firstnethou.com/annam/dancehis.html/index.html)

Jobs

The first immigrants were mainly farmers. Greeks are now active in running small businesses such as grocery stores, restaurants, bakeries, and coffeehouses.

Notable Greek Americans

Jennifer Aniston, actress.
Helene Alexopoulos, prima ballerina.
Bob Costas, sportscaster.
Michael Dukakis, governor of Massachusetts, 1974–1978 and 1982–1990. Candidate for the U.S. presidency in 1988.
Olympia Dukakis, actress and cousin of Michael Dukakis.
Arianna Huffington, columnist, bestselling author, and political activist.
Pete Sampras, tennis champion.
Telly Savalas, actor.
George Tenet, CIA director.

Food

Wedding foods include *baklava* (pastries) and *kourabiethes* (shortbread cookies). *Kolliva* is a cake of nuts, raisins, pomegranate seeds, sugar, and spices, covered with powdered sugar that is specially prepared for memorial services. *Dolmadia* is an appetizer of rice and cooked grape leaves. *Taramosalata* is another appetizer and is a combination of smoked cod roe and cooked potatoes that is a favorite among Greek food lovers. *Tiropita* is a type of cheese pie, and another variation of this pie is *spanakopita* (with spinach, as well as cheese). A very traditional Greek dish is *moussaka*, made with eggplants, ground beef, and grated cheese. *Souvlaki* is a main dish consisting of barbecued cubed meat (lamb, pork, or chicken) served with onions, tomatoes, and herbs, sometimes topped with *tzatziki*, a yogurt-based dressing with garlic and cucumbers. Pita bread and Greek salads (incorporating feta cheese) are also traditional.

Most Greek Americans today live in the metropolitan areas in which their great grandparents settled, such as Chicago and New York. Since Americans descended from Greeks are often fair-skinned—and even fairer if their ancestry includes other pale-skinned forebears—they blend with the white majority. Their religion, though distinctly Greek Orthodox Catholic, is familiar to other Catholics. Their children often attend Catholic schools with students of diverse ethnic backgrounds. What sets them apart is the Greek tradition remaining in their home lives. Typical Greek American families are close-knit and nurture their Greek heritage and its customs.

Greek Americans take an active interest in the politics of Greece and the United States. They have lobbied for many causes in their homeland. Their protests against the Turkish invasion in 1974 of Cyprus, a Mediterranean island whose population is 78 percent Greek Cypriot, played an important role in securing a U.S. arms embargo against Turkey in 1975.

Religion

The traditional Greek American religion is Greek Orthodox, the church stemming from the Greek-speaking Catholic church of the Byzantine Empire. Orthodoxy is the religion of Holy Communion, confession, and infant baptism. Orthodox Christians throughout the world use various ethnic or national titles such as Greek Orthodox, Russian Orthodox, Serbian Orthodox, or to be more general, Eastern Orthodox. However, the Greek Orthodox religion does not accept the authority of the pope and is known for its elaborate services and ancient customs. The word "Catholic" comes from the Greek word *katholikos*, which means "worldwide" or "universal."

Culture and Tradition

Dance is an important part of Greek culture. Many Greek dances have changed on American soil. One example is the fast Cretan Syrto dance, from western Crete. In the years after World War II Greeks in Pittsburgh, Pennsylvania, danced the authentic steps; but without the original Cretan music the dance became slower and is now performed to many different songs.

Greek American men and women in traditional dress perform a Greek dance.

Much Greek tradition survives at weddings. Greek Americans often dance the *hasapiko* and the *kalamatianos* in circles and lines. Wedding foods include pastries such as *baklava* and shortbread cookies called *kourabiethes*. Guests sometimes rent traditional Greek costumes. Attitudes toward intermarriage have relaxed in the past century, and marriages today are often mixed—six out of ten Greek American marriages in the 1980s were mixed. Other significant events carry important customs. Gifts of silver coins to newborns are for luck, and blue and black stones are meant to ward off evil. When a family member dies, Greek custom calls for men to wear a black armband for 40 days. However, it is rare today for Greek American women to follow the tradition of wearing black for that length of time.

Greece was home of the first ancient Olymic Games more than 2,000 years ago and of the first modern games in 1896. In 2004 Greece is again to play host to the 28th Olympiad in Athens.

See also

- Albanians (Volume 1)
- Religion (Volume 9)
- Turks (Volume 10)

Greenlanders

Greenland, the world's largest island, is located in northern North America between the Arctic Ocean and the North Atlantic Ocean. Glaciers cover 80 percent of the mountainous landmass, and the land is virtually treeless. The present population originated with Inuit groups who first occupied Greenland about 5,000 years ago. Colonized by the Danes in the 17th century, Greenland became part of Denmark in 1953. Since 1979 the island has been largely self-governing, and the right to full independence was granted in 1998. Of the current population of 59,309, the majority are Inuit, many of whom have relocated to urban areas since the 1960s. Only about 10,000 are Danish immigrants.

The economy is heavily subsidized by the Danish government and relies on fishing and fish processing, shrimping, animal herding (sheep and reindeer), hunting, mining, and tourism and ship construction. High unemployment levels and limited educational facilities have led some Greenlanders to seek opportunities abroad. Some live in Canada and the United States temporarily as workers, eventually returning to Greenland, while others settle permanently. In recent years this migration has mainly been of young people to the universities of Toronto and Montreal. Emigration to the United States is rarer, although cultural exchanges do take place, and students are encouraged to study at American colleges.

Greenlander culture

In addition to Danish, the Inuit of Greenland speak their own distinct language. Traditional activities like dog sledding, hiking, and kayaking remain popular today. Inuit culture emphasizes harmony with land and nature, and customs include dancing to spiritual songs and rhythmic drumming. The influence of Danish colonists can be seen in the architecture of local houses and in the wearing of woolen clothing.

See also

- Danes (Volume 3)
- Icelanders (Volume 5)
- Inuits (Volume 5)

Fact File: GREENLANDERS

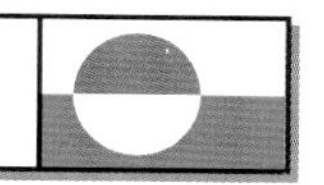

Region of origin

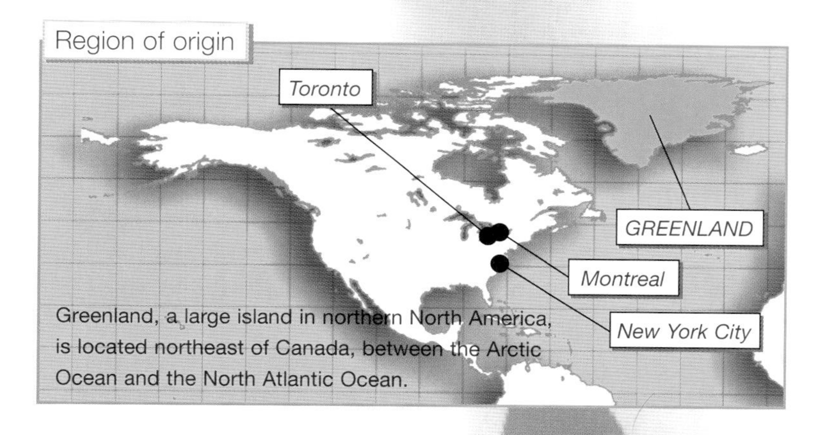

Greenland, a large island in northern North America, is located northeast of Canada, between the Arctic Ocean and the North Atlantic Ocean.

Population

U.S./Canada (2000 estimate): 2,000.

Distribution

Canada: Toronto and Montreal.
USA: New York City.

Language

Greenlandic (an East Inuit dialect), Danish, English.

Festivals

Mitaartut (On January 6 children dress in disguise and go out to knock on doors for treats).
End of the polar night (January or February).
Birthday of the Queen of Denmark (April 16).
Ullortuneq (June 21, the summer solstice).

Food

Walrus, seal and whale meat are traditional local staples, along with shrimp, fish (halibut and cod), lamb, reindeer, berries, and dairy products. They are supplemented with imported European and American foods. Greenlanders love to drink coffee.

Community organizations

Inuit Circumpolar Conference (www.inuitcircumpolar.com)
Royal Danish Embassy, Washington, D.C. (www.denmarkemb.org/greenland.htm)

Guatemalans

Guatemalan culture

Soccer is very popular among Guatemalan Americans, and they join soccer leagues with other Hispanic immigrants. The Maya Indians have their own distinctive traditions in music, dance, and weaving. They have tried to preserve their culture in their adopted homeland, particularly in view of the Guatemalan government's systematic destruction of their way of life. They celebrate many festivals, particularly the regional festivals of their home villages. Children are less likely to follow their parents' traditions and more likely to integrate into U.S. society.

Guatemala is the most densely populated country in Central America. Its peoples started emigrating to the United States largely from the late 1960s onward, following the outbreak of a long and violent civil war in their homeland in which indigenous villages were destroyed and their populations tortured, raped, and murdered by the right-wing army. The highest concentration of Guatemalan Americans is in California, particularly in established Hispanic communities in Los Angeles and San Francisco. The large number of illegal Guatemalan American immigrants settle in areas where they can remain anonymous. Many pretend to be Mexican so they can be deported to Mexico rather than back to Guatemala.

Guatemala has the highest indigenous population of all Central America (50 percent), and many of the immigrants come from one of the 22 groups of Mayan descent, each of which has its own language and culture. They speak their native languages at home and learn Spanish when they come to the United States. There are significant Kanjobal Indian communities in both California and Florida.

Migration Patterns

Guatemala is slightly smaller than the state of Tennessee, with a population of approximately 13 million. It is bordered by Belize, El Salvador, Honduras, and Mexico. Significant migration from Guatemala to the United States started with the CIA-backed overthrow of the democratically elected left-wing President Arbenz in 1954. Arbenz' radical program of land redistribution—which included redistributing the substantial holdings of the U.S.-owned United Fruit Company—brought him into conflict with the U.S. government.

Following the revolt, left-wing political activists, intellectuals, and educated middle-class Guatemalans began to leave the country. In the late 1960s and early 1970s, as the civil war escalated, the numbers of Guatemalans emigrating rose dramatically. Many of them came from the Indian population because of the Guatemalan government's systematic destruction of Indian villages. During the 1970s and 1980s the numbers of migrants, both legal and illegal, again soared.

Many sought political asylum in the United States, but the U.S. government was reluctant to grant asylum because, unlike the Nicaraguans, the Guatemalans were not fleeing a communist regime. By the end of 1995 there were still 125,867 Guatemalan American asylum cases outstanding, and more than 97 percent of the claimants that had been heard had been denied asylum status.

Guatemalan children at a refugee camp in Mexico. Civil unrest and political instability in Guatemala have meant that the numbers of those seeking an escape have risen steadily since the 1950s.

Communities in North America

The Guatemalan American community is drawn from different ethnic groups, and their lifestyles differ accordingly. The educated, urban middle-class Guatemalans (of European descent) integrate well into their local Hispanic and American communities. Conversely, the indigenous Guatemalans lack a formal school education, and many do not speak Spanish when they arrive in the United States. As a result, they rely heavily on the established local community. In the Chicago area Guatemalan Americans speak Maya languages, including Quiché, Kanjobal, Tzutuhil, and Pochonchi. In southern Florida there is a Kanjobal community from the Guatemalan village of San Miguel Acatlán who do not speak Spanish or have a written language. They work mainly in the Florida citrus fields.

Many Guatemalan Americans consider their stay in the United States to be temporary and plan to return home after they have saved enough money. In the meantime, they send money home. For all Guatemalans the family is crucial. Many leave family members behind in Guatemala, and their only contact is by telephone. Guatemalan women have more independence while they are in the United States than they do at home, largely because they earn their own money. However, many Guatemalans live on the poverty line. Those who are illegal migrants cannot claim welfare, and many work at low-paid jobs while living in crowded housing. Nevertheless, they strive to preserve their culture and identity, although that is becoming harder for those Guatemalan children born in the United States.

Guatemalan politics

Although it is difficult for some Guatemalan Americans to be politically active because of their illegal status, those who are legal migrants to the United States have lobbied for increased freedom back in Guatemala and for a recognition of the human rights abuses that have taken place there. In the United States changes in the immigration laws that meant a loss of welfare benefits led all Guatemalans who were eligible to register as U.S. citizens.

See also

- Belizeans (Volume 1)
- Illegal immigration (Volume 5)
- Mexicans (Volume 7)

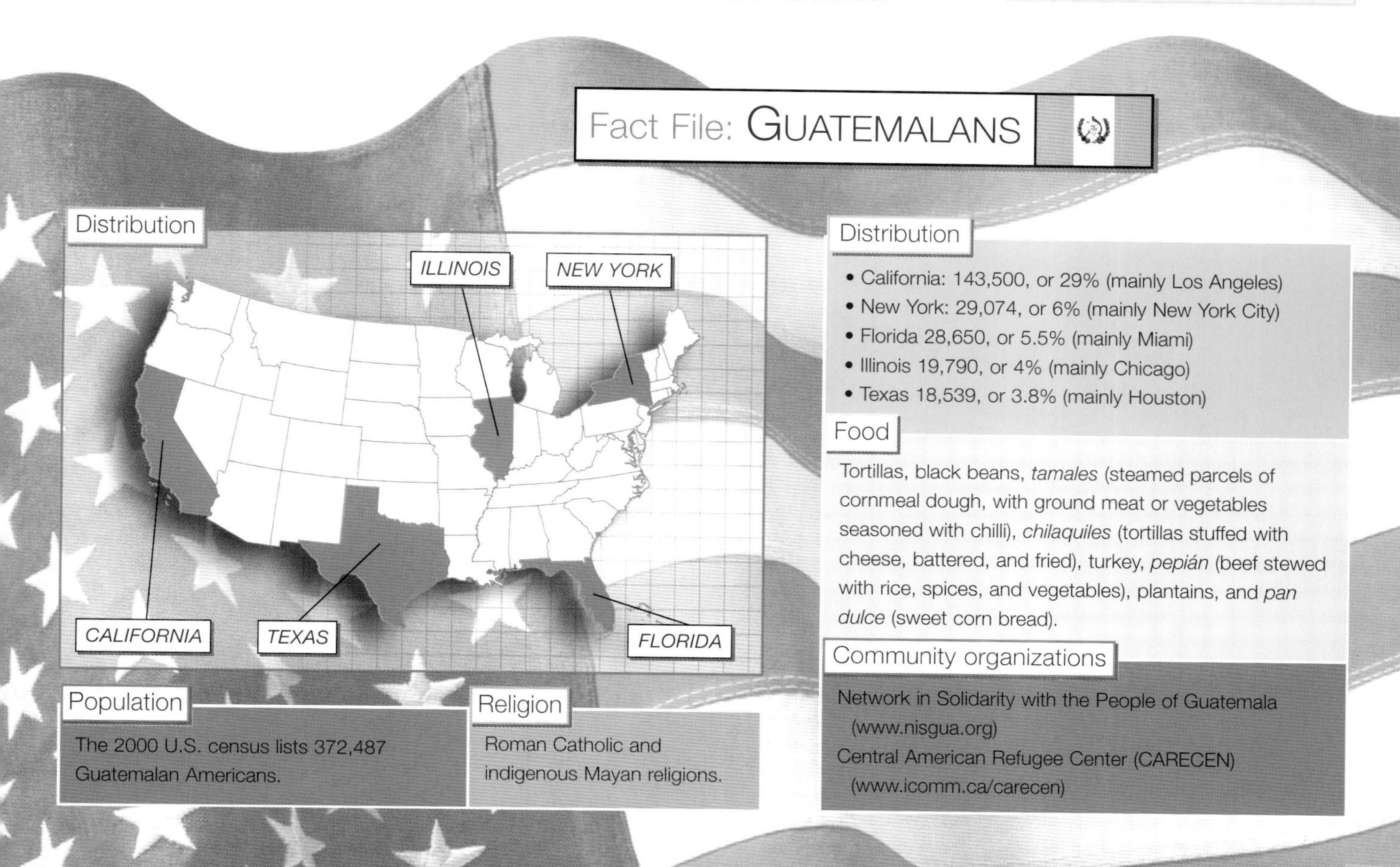

Fact File: GUATEMALANS

Distribution

- California: 143,500, or 29% (mainly Los Angeles)
- New York: 29,074, or 6% (mainly New York City)
- Florida 28,650, or 5.5% (mainly Miami)
- Illinois 19,790, or 4% (mainly Chicago)
- Texas 18,539, or 3.8% (mainly Houston)

Population

The 2000 U.S. census lists 372,487 Guatemalan Americans.

Religion

Roman Catholic and indigenous Mayan religions.

Food

Tortillas, black beans, *tamales* (steamed parcels of cornmeal dough, with ground meat or vegetables seasoned with chilli), *chilaquiles* (tortillas stuffed with cheese, battered, and fried), turkey, *pepián* (beef stewed with rice, spices, and vegetables), plantains, and *pan dulce* (sweet corn bread).

Community organizations

Network in Solidarity with the People of Guatemala (www.nisgua.org)
Central American Refugee Center (CARECEN) (www.icomm.ca/carecen)

Guyanese

> **Guyanese politics**
>
> Some Guyanese Americans, disillusioned with the Guyanese government, are actively lobbying to have Guyana incorporated into the United States. Immigrants become U.S. citizens as soon as they can on arrival—there are already more than 100,000 citizens of Guyanese extraction in the United States—and many others intend to follow as soon as they have fulfilled the immigration requirements. Colin Moore, a Guyanese American lawyer from Brooklyn, ran unsuccessfully for New York governor in 1994.

Guyanese Americans come from the only English-speaking country in South America. Guyana is situated in northeast South America. With a population of 780,000, it is slightly smaller than the U.S. state of Idaho and is the third poorest country in Latin America and the Caribbean.

Guyanese Americans are economic migrants who live mainly on the East Coast, with the highest concentration in the New York metropolitan area (80 percent), where they absorb easily into the established Caribbean community. Such has been the extent of immigration to the United States that there is a lobby among Guyanese Americans to see Guyana become part of the United States.

The Guyanese Nation

The Guyanese are a nation of immigrants and comprise many nationalities, predominantly East Indians, Africans, Chinese, and Europeans. Half the population is of East Indian origin, and 30 percent is of African origin. The country has a very low literacy rate. A recent survey found that up to 89 percent of school children were functionally illiterate, that is, they did not have the ability to effectively apply reading and writing skills in everyday situations. Lack of investment and reliance on traditional agricultural exports—sugar and rice—have led to economic stagnation in Guyana and an exodus of educated Guyanese.

Until independence in 1966 Guyana was part of the British Empire, and traditionally Guyanese moved to Britain. However, changes in U.S. immigration laws in 1952 resulted in a wave of migration to the United States that was compounded a decade later when Britain changed its immigration laws to discourage migration from its colonies. Educated, professional Guyanese workers could no longer find work in the United Kingdom and moved to the United States. As the Guyanese economy continued to stagnate in the 1970s and 1980s, more immigrants followed. They worked largely in healthcare and as domestic help. Since the 1960s more women than men have migrated. In 1980, of the 48,608 Guyanese migrants to the United States, 26,046 were women.

Miners and sugar plantation workers at a rally during the General Strike of 1945 in British Guiana, now Guyana. Independence from British colonial rule came in 1966, but political unrest continued.

Waves of Immigration

The earliest Guyanese immigrants to the United States arrived at the turn of the 19th and 20th centuries. They were mainly men who, along with other Caribbean migrants, moved to New York to work in sugar and coffee processing plants or to find employment in factories. The next wave of migration began in the 1950s and continues today. Like earlier Guyanese immigrants, these Guyanese tend to be hard workers who save their money to enable family members in Guyana to join them. The one significant change has been that many women now head households.

When immigrants arrive in the United States, they stay with family and friends until they find work. Then they move to boarding houses, often sharing cramped living conditions with other Guyanese and Caribbean immigrants.

Family and Social Life

Family is the center of the Guyanese American's life. They work in order to educate their children and to buy their own homes. Some Guyanese Americans educate their children privately because they welcome the added discipline. The church, particularly the Episcopalian church, plays an important part in Guyanese life, serving as a network for immigrants. Guyanese in the United States also have close links with other immigrant communities from the British Caribbean such as the Jamaicans and Barbadians.

See also

- African Americans (Volume 1)
- Asian Indians (Volume 1)
- Brazilians (Volume 2)
- Caribbean peoples (Volume 2)
- Hispanic Americans (Volume 5)
- Venezuelans (Volume 10)

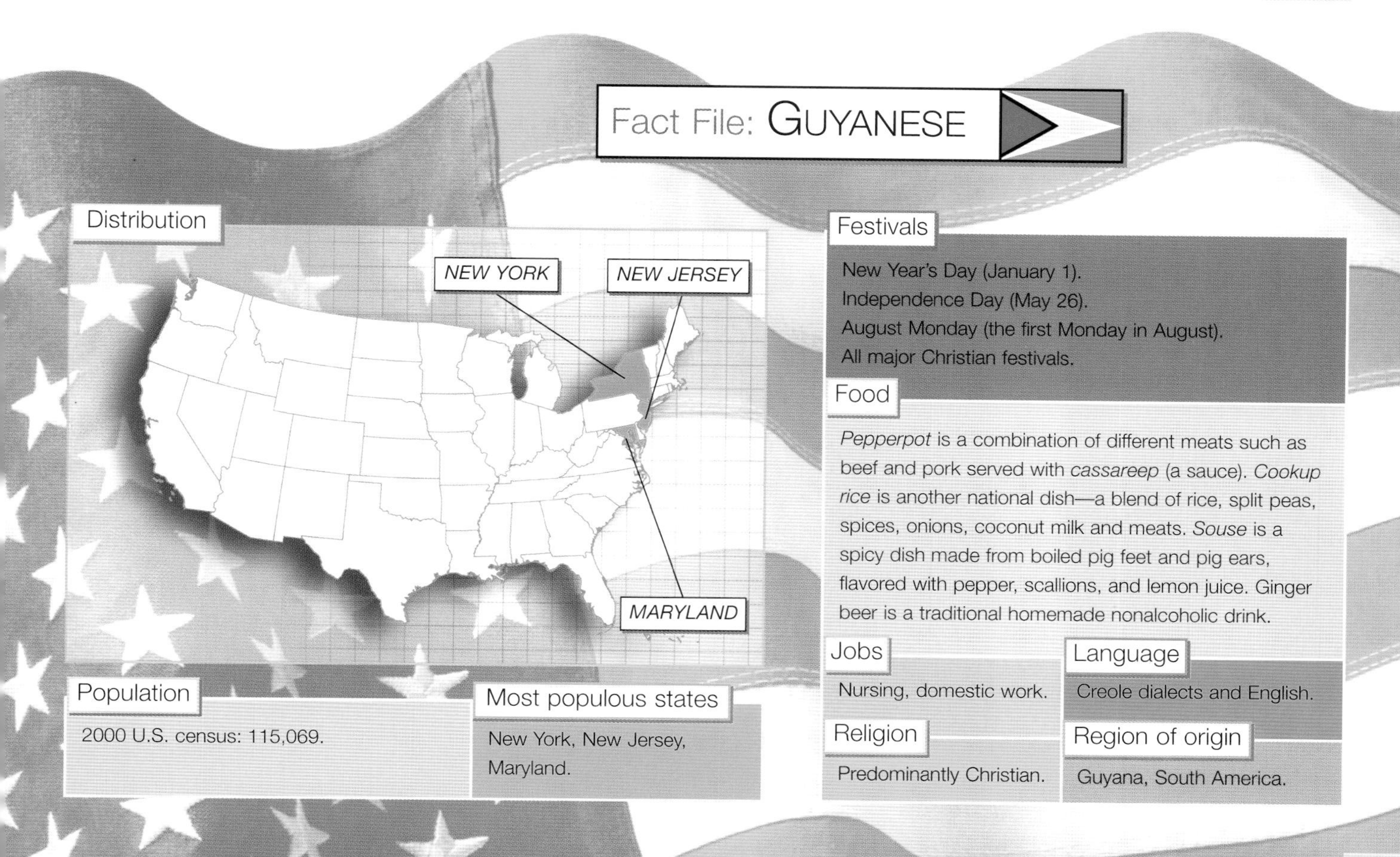

Glossary

affirmative action government programs to provide equal opportunities to minority groups.

alien a foreign-born resident who has not been naturalized and is still a subject or citizen of another country.

assimilation the process by which an individual or a minority group adopts the values and practices of the dominant culture and loses its own cultural distinctiveness.

asylum the legal status granted to a foreign individual who fears political persecution if he or she is forced to return home.

bilingualism the ability to speak fluently in two languages.

census a comprehensive survey of a population designed to gather basic demographic information. In the United States the census is carried out every 10 years.

citizen a native or foreign-born member of a country who has legal and political rights within that country.

colony a territory ruled by another country.

cultural mingling a process that occurs when two or more cultures come into contact and interact with one another.

cultural retention the process by which an immigrant group or individual retains elements of their native heritage in a new society.

deportation the legal removal of an immigrant from a country.

diaspora the historical dispersal of a group of people of similar origins from their homeland to many lands.

discrimination the unfair denial of equal rights or opportunities to a group or individual based on cultural, social, or racial differences.

emigrant a person who leaves his or her homeland to live in a foreign country.

emigration the movement of people from their homeland to another country.

emigré a person forced to emigrate for political reasons.

ethnic group a group sharing common origins and cultural similarities, such as beliefs, values, customs, and language, geography, kinship, or race.

ethnicity identification with and inclusion within an ethnic group.

exclusion act a law passed to refuse entry into the United States to a certain race or nationality.

ghetto an often deprived urban area occupied predominantly by members of a single race or ethnic group.

immigrant a person who moves to a country other than his or her homeland.

immigration the settlement of people in a country other than that in which they were born.

indigenous a term referring to the original inhabitants of a land or territory.

integration the mixing of different racial groups within a community.

melting pot a phrase coined by Jewish playwright Israel Zangwill to refer to America's multicultural society in the early 20th century.

middle class a socioeconomic class broadly defined as those with middle income working in mental rather than manual occupations.

migrant a term describing someone who regularly moves from one place to another, often for economic reasons.

migration the movement of people from one country to settle in another.

minority group a subgroup of society characterized by factors including race, religion, nationality, gender, or culture.

multiethnic a term meaning belonging not to one single racial or ethnic group but to two or more.

multiculturalism a positive attitude toward cultural diversity that supports the right of ethnic groups to maintain their cultural distinctiveness within the dominant culture.

nativism an anti-immigrant U.S. political tradition, popular in the 19th century, that valued "real" Americans and their attitudes over more recent immigrants.

naturalization the legal process by which a foreign person becomes a citizen of a country with the same rights as a native-born citizen.

pluralism the equal coexistence of diverse ethnic groups within a single society.

prejudice the holding of unfounded ideas about groups or individuals based on negative stereotypes.

quota (system) a limit on the number of immigrants from particular countries allowed into another.

race the classification of people based on genetic characteristics or common nationality, history, or experiences.

racism discrimination against others based on an assumption of one's own racial superiority.

refugee a term referring to a person who lives in a foreign country to escape persecution at home.

repatriation the forcible or voluntary return of immigrants to their country of origin.

segregation the discriminatory separation or isolation of ethnic, social, or religious groups, for example, in restricted areas such as ghettos.

slavery the ownership of human beings by others.

social mobility the movement of groups or individuals within the social hierachy.

stereotype a usually negative categorization of all individuals within a group based on a rigid and inflexible image of the characteristics of that group.

upper class the more affluent members of society, especially those who have great wealth or hold an esteemed position in society.

urban renewal the rebuilding of deteriorating city neighborhoods, often those that have become ghettos.

working class a social group made up broadly of people in manual occupations.

Further reading

Ansari, Maboud. ***The Making of the Iranian Community in America.*** New York: Pardis Press, 1993.

Avery, Donald. ***Reluctant Host: Canada's Response to Immigrant Workers 1896–1994.*** Toronto: McClelland & Stewart, 1995.

Axtell, James. ***Natives and Newcomers: The Cultural Origins of North America.*** New York: Oxford University Press, 2000.

Barry, Brian M. ***Culture and Equality: An Egalitarian Critique of Multiculturalism.*** Cambridge, MA: Harvard University Press, 2001.

Bodnar, John. ***The Transplanted: A History of Immigrants in Urban America (Interdisciplinary Studies in History).*** Bloomington, IN: Indiana University Press, 1987.

Brown, Dee Alexander. ***Bury My Heart at Wounded Knee: An Indian History of the American West.*** New York: Henry Holt and Company, 2001 revised edition.

Capp, Diana White Horse. ***Brother against Brother: America's New War over Land Rights.*** Bellevue, WA: Merril Press, 2002.

Chavez, Leo R. ***Shadowed Lives: Undocumented Immigrants in American Society.*** Belmont, CA: Wadsworth Pub, 1997.

Ciongoli, A. Kenneth, and Jay Parini. ***Passage to Liberty: The Story of Italian Immigration and the Rebirth of America.*** New York: Regan Books, HarperCollins, 2002.

Connell-Szasz, Margaret (ed.). ***Between Indian and White Worlds: The Cultural Broker.*** Norman, OK: University of Oklahoma Press, 1994.

Daniel Tatum, Beverly. ***Assimilation Blues: Black Families in a White Community.*** Boulder, CO: Basic Books, 2000.

Dezell, Maureen. ***Irish America: Coming into Clover.*** New York: Doubleday, 2001.

Diner, Hasia R. ***Jewish Americans: The Immigrant Experience.*** Southport, CT: Hugh Lauter Levin Assoc., 2002.

Do, Hien Duc. ***The Vietnamese Americans.*** Westport, CT: Greenwood Press, 2000.

Flores, Juan. ***Divided Borders: Essays on Puerto Rican Identity.*** Houston, TX: Arte Publico Press, 1993.

Franklin, John Hope, and Alfred A. Moss. ***From Slavery to Freedom: A History of African Americans.*** New York: Alfred A. Knopf, 2000.

Frye Jacobson, Matthew. ***Whiteness of a Different Color: European Immigrants and the Alchemy of Race.*** Cambridge, MA: Harvard University Press, 1999.

Getis, Arthur, Judith Getis, and I. E. Quastler (eds.). ***The United States and Canada: The Land and the People.*** New York: McGraw-Hill, 2000.

Gonzalez, Juan. ***Harvest of Empire: A History of Latinos in America.*** New York: Viking Press, 2000.

Gonzalez-Pando, Miguel. ***The Cuban Americans.*** Westport, CT: Greenwood Press, 1998.

Govorchin, Gerald Gilbert. ***From Russia to America with Love: A Study of the Russian Immigrants in the United States.*** Pittsburgh, PA: Dorrance Publishing, 1993.

Grimes, Kimberly M. ***Crossing Borders: Changing Social Identities in Southern Mexico.*** Tucson, AZ: University of Arizona Press, 1998.

Hegi, Ursula. ***Tearing the Silence: Being German in America.*** New York: Simon & Schuster, 1997.

Hilfiker, David. ***Urban Injustice: How Ghettos Happen.*** New York: Seven Stories Press, 2002.

Horn, Michiel. ***Becoming Canadian: Memoirs of an Invisible Immigrant.*** Toronto: University of Toronto Press, 1997.

Inada, Lawson Fusao (ed.). ***Only What We Could Carry: The Japanese American Internment Experience.*** Berkeley, CA: Heyday Books, 2000.

Kelley, Ninette, and Michael J. Trebilcock. ***The Making of the Mosaic: The History of Canadian Immigration Policy.*** Toronto: University of Toronto Press, 1998.

Kelly, Paul. ***Multiculturalism Reconsidered: Culture and Equality and Its Critics.*** Cambridge, England: Polity Press, 2003.

Kibria, Nazli. ***Becoming Asian American: Second-Generation Chinese and Korean American Identities.*** Baltimore, MD: Johns Hopkins University Press, 2002.

Lehman, Jeffrey (ed.). ***Gale Encyclopedia of Multicultural America.*** Detroit, MI: Gale Research, Inc., 2000.

Miscevic, Dusanka, and Peter Kwong. ***Chinese Americans: The Immigrant Experience.*** Southport, CT: Hugh Lauter Levin Assoc., 2000.

Morton Coan, Peter. ***Ellis Island Interviews: In Their Own Words.*** New York: Facts on File, 1997.

Naff, Alixa. ***The Arab Americans.*** Broomall, PA: Chelsea House, 1998.

Portes, Alejandro, and Rubén G. Rumbaut (eds.). ***Ethnicities: Children of Immigrants in America.*** Los Angeles, CA: University of California Press, 2001.

Stoffman, Daniel. ***Who Gets In: What's Wrong with Canada's Immigration Program—And How to Fix It.*** Toronto: Macfarlane Walter & Ross, 2002.

Takaki, Ronald. ***Strangers from a Different Shore: A History of Asian Americans.*** New York: Back Bay Books, 1998.

Thernstrom, Stephan A., Ann Orlov, and Oscar Handlin (eds.). ***Harvard Encyclopedia of American Ethnic Groups***. Cambridge, MA: Belknap Press, 1980.

Waldinger, Roger (ed.). ***Strangers at the Gates: New Immigrants in Urban America.*** Los Angeles, CA: University of California Press, 2001.

Winks, Robin W. ***The Blacks in Canada: A History.*** Montreal: McGill-Queens University Press, 1997.

Relevant websites are listed separately with each entry.

Immigration timeline

1492 Christopher Columbus sails to North America

1534 Jacques Cartier sails up the St. Lawrence River

1535 Spain establishes colonial government in Mexico

1607 Settlers from England establish a colony in Jamestown, Virginia

1776 Declaration of Independence

1795 Naturalization Act restricts U.S. citizenship to "free white males" who reside in the United States for five years

1798 Alien and Sedition Act allows deportation of "dangerous" foreigners. Naturalization Act increases the residency requirement to 14 years

1802 Congress reduces residency requirement from 14 years to four

1808 Congress bans importation of slaves

1819 Steerage Acts: data collected on immigration for the first time

1820 Chinese arrive in California

1830 Indian Removal Act forces Native Americans to give up their lands east of the Mississippi River

1834 Slavery abolished in British North America (Canada)

1840s Major immigration of Irish and Germans due to crop failures

1846 Mexican–American War starts

1848 Mexican–American War ends. United States purchases New Mexico, Arizona, California, Utah, Nevada, and Texas

1850 Fugitive Slave Act

1860s Mass immigration from Poland

1861 American Civil War begins

1862 American Homestead Act provides settlers with free land in the Midwest

1863 Emancipation Proclamation frees slaves in Union-held territory

1865 American Civil War ends; all slaves freed

1868 The Fourteenth Amendment endows slaves with citizenship. Japanese laborers arrive in Hawaii

1870 The Fifteenth Amendment: African American males given the right to vote

1880s Mass immigration from Italy. Civil unrest and economic instability throughout Russia

1882 Chinese Exclusion Act

1887 The Dawes Act dissolves many Indian reservations in United States

1890s Start of mass immigration of Ukrainians to Canada

1891 Polygamists, the sick, and those convicted of "moral turpitude" made ineligible for immigration

1892 Ellis Island opens

1896 Supreme Court rules that "separate but equal" facilities for blacks and whites are constitutional

1898 The Spanish–American War begins. U.S. acquisition of Puerto Rico and Guam

1900 Jones Act grants U.S. citizenship to Puerto Ricans

1901 Anarchist Exclusion Act

1907 Expatriation Act. "Gentleman's Agreement" curtails Japanese immigration

1910 Mexican Revolution begins: thousands of Mexicans flee to the United States

1917 The United States enters World War I

1918 World War I ends

1921 Quota Act restricts the immigration of southern and eastern Europeans

1924 Johnson–Reed Act reduces fixed quota to 2 percent of nationality groups. Oriental Exclusion Act limits immigration from East Asia. U.S. Border Control created

1929 Congress makes annual immigration quotas permanent

1930s Mass deportation of Mexicans during the Great Depression

1939 World War II begins

1940 Alien Registration Act requires registration and fingerprinting of aliens

1942 Japanese Americans moved to "relocation camps." Bracero Program allows Mexican laborers to work in the United States

1943 Magnuson Act repeals Chinese Exclusion Act of 1882

1945 World War II ends.

1948 Displaced Persons Act permits European war refugees entry to the United States

1950 Internal Security Act bars entry of communists to the United States. Korean War begins

1952 McCarran–Walter Immigration Act removes race as a basis for exclusion

1953 Congress amends the 1948 refugee policy to admit more refugees. Korean War ends

1954 U.S. Supreme Court rules that "separate but equal" educational facilities are unconstitutional. Operation Wetback: INS deports more than 3 million people of Mexican heritage

1959 Cuban revolution

1962 Amendments to Canada's Immigration Act eliminate racial and religious discrimination

1964 Civil Rights Acts

1965 Immigration Act ends quota system. Bracero Program ends. Vietnam War begins

1966 Cuban Refugee Act admits more than 400,000 people to the United States

1971 Canadian government officially endorses policy of multiculturalism

1975 Vietnam War ends: mass immigration from Vietnam

1980 Refugee Act: 10 million permanent immigrants are legally admitted to the United States

1986 The Immigration Reform and Control Act (IRCA) raises annual immigration ceiling to 540,000

1990 Immigration Act allows 700,000 immigrants per year into the United States

1991 Persian Gulf War

1995 Canada officially endorses policy of First Nations self-government

1996 Immigration Act mandates the building of fences on U.S.–Mexico border

2002 Department of Homeland Security established

2003 U.S. forces attack Iraq

Set index

Numbers in **bold** refer to volume numbers; those in *italics* refer to picture captions.

Picture credits

Front cover: Getty Images: American Stock; **background image: Corbis:** Bettmann. **Corbis**: 33; Bettmann 8, 13, 39; Jacques M. Chenet 23; Howard Davies 4; Sandy Felsenthal 25; Philip Gould 38; Farrell Grehan 14; Kelly-Mooney Photography 58; Layne Kennedy 35; Bob Kirst 24; Dorothea Lange 27; Michael S. Lewis 5; Gunter Marx 64; Bob Rowan 61; Lee Snider 55; Ted Spiegel 20; David & Peter Turnley 6, 66; Michael S. Yamashita 30; **Getty Images**: 18, 43, 50, 68; American Stock 49, 53; Baron 51; Luis Casteneda Inc 47; Evans 45; Ernst Haas 7; Lewis W. Hine 19, 21; Patrick J. LaCroix 46; William Lippincott 44; Rita Maas 40; Pet 57; George Pickow 22; Arthur Rothstein 62; **Kobal Collection**: 15, 37; **Library of Congress**: 31; **National Archives**: 36; **Peter Newark's American Pictures**: 11t, 11b, 41, 56; **Photos 12**: 32; **Rex Features**: Peter Brooker 29; Erick C. Pendzich 26; **Robert Hunt Library**: 9, 12, 59, 60.